DANCING *in the* FOUNTAIN

How to Enjoy Living Abroad

What fun. You will laugh and play and eat and connect . . . McCann's wacky sense of humor will have you smiling on every page. Just reading this will give you the confidence of an experienced traveler. Happy journey.

— Rita Golden Gelman, *Tales of a Female Nomad*

Dancing in the Fountain is perhaps the best book about travel that I have ever read. It is certainly the best book about living — and living out loud — that I have ever read. It is full of wry humor and it is laugh-out-loud funny — the adventure with the snake, to mention just one. And it includes many of life's bittersweet moments, such as discovering that long-time friends are really just geographically convenient, that expats move on and that favourite dogs don't live forever. Unless you are determined never to step foot outside your own town, this is an author you will really want to know and a book you will really want to read. I read this in one sitting. I could not do otherwise, but I will go back again and again for the philosophical insights.

— Guy Thatcher, *A Journey of Days*

Dancing in the Fountain . . . is filled with the hard-won lessons of coping (those crazy bureaucrats who keep you filling out forms for eternity to get your visa; those numbskulls who seem to have misplaced your dog in the airport) and the continuing pleasures of living abroad (tapas at midnight, flamenco, dancing in the fountain!). And of course, the hazards of messing up in a new language – "Yes, please do take my leg off," when what you really meant was "Yes, please remove my plate." Mostly, this read is a hoot, filled with great humor and insight."

— Joanna Biggar, *That Paris Year*

Karen McCann's witty, fresh and engaging new book, *Dancing in the Fountain*, captures the charming unpredictability of life in Andalucía. Seen through her eyes, creating a new life in an old European city has never been so delightful, heartwarming and laugh-out-loud funny.

— Victoria Twead, *Chickens, Mules and Two Old Fools*

A witty, fast-moving account of expats living in Spain, with all the excitement that comes with getting to grips with a new language and culture. Expats will recognize it and laugh along with the author, others will be moved to give it a try. Karen McCann's sharp eye for detail brings the city of Seville to life.

— Joan Fallon, *Daughters of Spain*

Karen McCann arrived in Sevilla with a very dry sense of humour and a road wisdom earned from volunteering in hot spots around the world. Her story of her feet-first immersion in its culture had me pining for the Alcázar gardens and the street life of my favourite Spanish city. If you share her open heart and mind, you too might become an adopted Sevillano.

— John Gill, *Andalucía: A Cultural History*

If you've been waiting for a sign from the universe to live where you've always dreamed of living, consider the book *Dancing in the Fountain* your sign to go ahead and do it. Yes, you have permission to live your dream! You also have permission to sit in a comfy chair and be there through Karen McCann's fascinating and laugh-out-loud story. Either way, readers will enjoy dipping their toes in both foreign and domestic fountains.

— Nancy Solak, *A Footpath in Umbria*

Dancing in the Fountain is a 'new life in Spain' book with a difference. Funny, informative and well written, it skips along at a pace, giving the reader a real feel for Seville and the Spanish way of life, warts and all. Karen's enthusiasm for her life in Spain and the Spanish culture shines through. A thoroughly enjoyable read!

— June Wolfe, *No Time for a Siesta*

DANCING *in the* FOUNTAIN

How to Enjoy Living Abroad

Karen McCann

CAFÉ
SOCIETY
PRESS

Printed in the United States of America
First Printing, August 2012

Café Society Press
Chess Corporation
25825 Science Park Drive, Suite 100
Beachwood, Ohio 44122

enjoylivingabroad@gmail.com
www.enjoylivingabroad.com

ISBN: 0985028300
ISBN-13: 9780985028305

For Rich.
Thanks for the dance.

CONTENTS

PREFACE

❦

When I was growing up, my friends and I used to ask each other, "If you could live anywhere in the world, where would it be?" We'd then spend hours discussing the rival merits of Paris, London, Rome, and anyplace else we could think of that came under the thrilling and glamorous heading of "abroad." Years later, sitting in a dimly lit San Francisco restaurant on my first date with my husband-to-be, the subject came up again. Rich said, "I'd like to live abroad for a year. What do you think about Singapore?" I knew then that he was a keeper.

As it turned out, instead of Singapore, we went to live in Cleveland.

Two weeks after we came back from our honeymoon in the jungles of Costa Rica, a Cleveland firm made Rich an offer no sane person would have refused, and off we went. My sisters were appalled. Our San Francisco friends started referring to us in the past tense and wondering aloud if we'd done something terrible in a past life to deserve our fate. "Costa Rica?" said an old friend of Rich's. "Cleveland? When are you going to stop testing this woman?"

But as it happened, I loved Cleveland (yes, I did!). I had moved around a lot over the years, propelled by fluctuations in the family fortunes and later my own, and I had learned that I could make a good life for myself practically anywhere. One thing I know to be true: the secret is mentally unpacking your bags. Or, as the Buddhists like to put it, being here now.

In my Cleveland days, "here" was an old stone house on a wooded bluff overlooking a river, and "now" was a life filled with interesting work and great friends. We lived twenty-five miles outside the city, in a semirural area with woods, farms, and a large Amish community. We were deep in the American heartland, about as far from "abroad" as you can get.

But Rich always makes good on his promises, and a mere twenty years later, we moved to southern Spain. It began nearly eleven years ago with a visit to a friend's timeshare on the Mediterranean coast, which led to a return visit the following spring to study Spanish. That's when we took a side trip to Seville and found it too intriguing simply to pass through for a couple of days. We spent four spring vacations in Seville, staying for longer and longer periods, until finally we decided to move there "for a year." We've now been living in Seville for six and a half years, in a slightly crumbling old apartment overlooking the sun-bleached tile roof of an eighteenth-century church. A few years back we sold our beloved Cleveland house and bought a cottage in a small town north of San Francisco, near family and longtime friends, to serve as our home base when we're in the US. But most of our time is spent in Seville, and I'm still astonished at my good fortune.

And here's what I've learned: living abroad is easier than you think.

People often say to me, "You have the best of both worlds." (Wistful sigh.) "I wish I could do what you do." Half the time, I know perfectly well that my lifestyle wouldn't suit them at all.

They've chosen a different path and are just enjoying the kind of fleeting fantasy that comes with reading about people in wildly different circumstances, like Victorian London or outer space, and trying the idea on for size. After a few seconds, they're only too happy to set aside the fantasy to go back to browsing the Kindle store, helping the kids with their homework, or writing an email to colleagues.

But for anyone who might be seriously interested, I'll just say again, it's easier than you think. Of course, moving abroad — or anywhere, for that matter — has its challenges and will take time and effort to plan and carry out. But you don't have to wait until all the stars are aligned, the dog passes away, your grandkids are all happily married with good jobs, and you win the lottery.

Many people are under the impression that living abroad is terribly expensive — and it can be, if you buy a penthouse in the best neighborhood in Paris or Rome. But if you rent a comfortable apartment in a small, affordable city like Seville, your cost of living may actually go down or, as in our case, remain about the same. Although we pay a bit more in airfares every year, our basic expenses (housing, food, clothing, entertainment, ground transportation) are far more modest in Seville than when we made our home in Cleveland. Among other economies, we live in a walking city and don't need a car to get about. Without the car payments, insurance, garage fees, and maintenance, to say nothing of parking tickets, we can easily afford to hop a bus, rent a car, or take a taxi on those rare occasions when we need to.

Moving abroad may not have to wait until you're retired, either. While not every career can be uprooted and taken with you, I have friends in their twenties, thirties, and forties, often with large dogs and/or small children, who have figured out how to work successfully from a foreign base. In these technologically advanced times, all it takes is a computer to manage projects with business associates, keep tabs on investments, and stay in touch with family and friends in other countries. In fact, between Facebook and other media, I am now more familiar with the minutiae of my loved ones' lives than I was when we lived on the same block or even in the same house. And my initial concerns about missing family and friends evaporated when I learned that when you live in a destination city like Seville, *they* come to *you.* Sometimes the biggest challenge is getting them to leave again — but more about that later.

And contrary to what we've all read in so many charming books about Provence and Tuscany, it turns out that when you move to Europe, you are not actually required to purchase a crumbling old farmhouse in the country and spend years restoring it with the help of semiliterate but wise and amusing locals. That's a great life for some, but I find the country and suburbs to be very isolating, especially in a place like southern Spain, where people are slow to befriend anyone they haven't known since baptism. To me, it's infinitely more agreeable to rent an already-restored apartment in the center of a destination city, where the locals are more open to meeting foreigners and there's a lively and diverse international community. During my twenty years in Ohio, I spent more than enough evenings sitting on the back porch listening to the crickets. Now I'm delighted to be able to stroll around the corner to a flamenco show, wine tasting, or concert any night of the week and go out afterwards to a tapas bar with friends.

While you don't have to be wealthy, retired, or willing to restore a crumbling farmhouse to enjoy living abroad, there are some things you *will* need. The first is a good sense of humor, which is essential to surviving the general upheaval of any major life change, and most especially the social and linguistic pratfalls you'll inevitably be taking. Every foreign language is studded with little trip wires, such as the Spanish word *embarazada,* which sounds so much like the English "embarrassed," but in fact means "pregnant," creating endless opportunities for misunderstandings and faux pas. Or there's the common word *huevos,* literally "eggs" but often used as a slang word for testicles. You'll want to be very careful not to ask the guy at the farmers' market whether he has eggs; he'll inevitably reply "Yes, two big ones," and everyone within earshot will fall about laughing until you flee in confusion and have to find someplace else to buy your breakfast groceries.

An adaptable attitude is also a great help when living abroad. Naturally we all make comparisons with our country of origin, but it's best to avoid constantly demanding that other countries measure up to our standards and norms. I recently read a blog called "A Fantasy About Retiring Abroad," in which a financial planner weighed the pros and cons of living in a foreign country. Her conclusion was that it would be utterly impossible for her (and, she implied, anyone with any sense) to live in Europe because the Europeans do not have a "can-do" attitude and frequently fail to meet American efficiency standards. Oh honey, I wanted to tell her, that's the best reason I can think of *for* living in Europe. It's such a relief to live among people who value other things — such as family, friends, slow-cooked meals, witty and intimate conversation — above optimizing time management. It says a lot about our culture that this financial planner couldn't even have a *fantasy* that failed to achieve productivity benchmarks.

Respect for other cultures is essential too. There are times when all of us find it difficult to let go of preconceived notions of how things ought to work, especially in a foreign business setting. As part of our volunteer work for various organizations assisting struggling microenterprises, in the late 1990s Rich and I went to the former Soviet republic of Georgia. At the end of a fat dossier on the company's issues our case manager advised, "Don't write your report on the plane en route to the assignment." He was so right. One of my first suggestions for our clients was a mail marketing campaign. That's when I discovered that the nation's mail system hadn't functioned since the Soviets pulled out.

"Then how do you send out your bills?" I asked.

"We drive to people's homes. And while the bill collector is inside, the driver spray-paints our phone number on the wall of the building."

"And people don't object to that?" I asked incredulously. In the US there would be a lawsuit filed before the paint was dry.

"No, they like having the number handy." Apparently the phone books and directory assistance service had gone the way of the mail system.

I had to admit it was a great solution. Clearly my clients had a lot to teach me about marketing in the republic of Georgia.

And that's the whole fun of living abroad. You aren't doing things the same old way. You can't. Which means you're going to have to be open to new ways of thinking about *everything*.

Exploring new ways of approaching life can become addictive. "Abroad" is a very big place, and the possibilities are so intriguing that it's often hard to stop browsing and choose where you'd like to live. No matter how comfortably settled we are, Rich can never resist looking at real estate, and he automatically checks out housing prices wherever we travel so he can have the fun of imagining us living there.

"Listen to this," he said once, while reading a newspaper in the Himalayan kingdom of Bhutan. "You can get a three-bedroom house, with garden and toilet, for just four hundred thousand ngultrums. That's less than ten thousand dollars."

Reading the ad over his shoulder, I replied, "Yes, and it's conveniently located in downtown Wangdue Phodrang — which is where exactly?"

Rich had to admit that living in a small market town in central Bhutan might not give us the lifestyle we wanted, even with such bonus extras as garden and toilet.

Before our move to Seville, whenever we saw this kind of alluring real estate deal I would remind Rich of our agreement that we would never seriously consider living anywhere that we hadn't visited three times. We didn't want to make a move we'd repent at leisure. Like most Americans, I grew up on stories of immigrant forebears who left behind everyone and everything they knew forever in order to forge a new life in a new land. I find it immensely comforting to know that today you can try out places before you commit to them, and you can keep your ties to the old country in case things don't work out or just because you enjoy them both.

For me, things did work out. This is the story of why I moved to Seville and how I shaped a new life in a foreign country while maintaining a place for myself in my native land. My story will, I hope, provide you with some ideas about how you might experience living abroad, if you ever decide to try it. It is possible — fun, even — to engage in a whole new culture, face up to its challenges, and build a life that's truly yours in a country that isn't. And we're lucky enough to live in an age where you can do all that without cutting your ties to your homeland.

This book describes my adventures and misadventures in Seville, but the lessons I've learned can be applied to any international move, whether it's to a bungalow in India, a flat in Moscow, or a *mieszkanie* in Warsaw. I've devoted chapters to the topics that people most often ask me about: learning a foreign language, finding housing, bringing along your beloved pet, making friends, adapting to unfamiliar eating and drinking customs, dealing with a very different health care system, and coping with the arrival of more houseguests than you could ever have imagined possible. The book focuses largely on my experiences in Seville, but you'll also be hearing about my life in the US — in Cleveland and California — to provide context for my stories and to give you a realistic idea of how you, too, might be able to structure a good life that embraces the old as well as the new.

You'll learn about friends I made (some of whom appear here under other names, out of respect for their privacy) and mistakes I blundered into along the way. One of the great things about living abroad is that you have countless new ways to screw up, providing many valuable opportunities for honing your wits and your sense of the ridiculous. We've all read articles about how to keep your brain's synapses firing by doing Sudoku, taking up knitting, or going bird watching, but frankly, I find life in a foreign country to be a far more interesting and effective way to stay sharp. The French writer Émile Zola once said, "If you ask me what I came into the world to do, I will tell you: I came to live out loud." And if you ask me, I will tell you there's nothing quite like going abroad to pump up the volume on your life.

Chapter 1

KNOW WHEN TO GO

Not long after I moved to Seville, I watched a well-dressed, middle-aged Spaniard stop as if thunderstruck in front of a restaurant's display window. He stood gazing rapturously at three enormous sea bass suspended over a bed of ice, their great silver bodies arched as if leaping toward the glass, teeth bared in a hunter's fierce grin. Suddenly the Spaniard burst into song. And not just any song, but a passionate *saeta*, the "arrow" of melody that is launched at the Blessed Virgin from balconies during the holiest of the spring processions. To this man, beholding magnificent fish was a form of religious ecstasy.

And I said to myself, for perhaps the hundredth time, "And that's why I live here."

The Sevillanos consider it their God-given birthright to enjoy themselves and their city. They fling themselves into their social lives with the same zeal Americans devote to their careers. Just meeting a friend for a *café con leche* can take two hours, not counting the preliminary debate about where to go for the best coffee at the best price. Lunch is even more time-consuming; my record so far is seven hours one St. Patrick's Day in an Italian restaurant on the Costa del Sol. Dinners may last until four in the morning. Late nights can run until dawn and not infrequently include walking home through the silent streets, arm in arm with friends, and (if I am to be totally honest with you) singing a medley of old show tunes, Beatles hits, and Bésame Mucho. The neighbors put up with it because they know that next time, they could be the ones serenading the barrio.

Of course, you have to work your way up to this kind of lifestyle. A little over ten years ago, when I first visited Seville, I was living a much quieter life in a sleepy little town outside of Cleveland: writing for regional magazines, doing a bit of consulting, volunteering with the local fire department and various charities. My husband, Rich, had recently taken early retirement after decades of fourteen-hour days in a high-stress environment. He kept up a small consulting practice, often with projects involving us both, but for much of the time he was living his dream of spending his days working the land. He was up with the sun every morning, tending the vegetable garden and carving yet another lovely, labor-intensive flower bed out of the front lawn. During the spring planting and fall harvest, I was recruited to serve as assistant gardener, and we toiled like fourteenth-century peasants, backs bent in the muddy fields from dawn to dusk, racing against the short Ohio growing season. Then winter would set in, and after working his way through the seed catalogs, Rich would start reading travel brochures.

For many years we escaped the depths of the Midwest winter to visit such steamy locales as Thailand, Vietnam, and Belize. Occasionally we took volunteer work assignments in Bosnia, El Salvador, and elsewhere; twice we spent the late winter months in the old Soviet republic of Georgia, working with medical clinics struggling to make the shift to the capitalist system in a semicollapsed economy. We loved visiting new places, even while shivering in an unheated Georgian office building or sweltering in a bamboo hut with pigs and dogs fighting over our food scraps just outside the door. Rich and I often talked about living abroad "someday," but it was always a long way off, somewhere between the unforeseeable future and a never-to-be-realized fantasy.

Around the time Rich took early retirement, many of our older friends were collecting their pensions and buying condos in warmer places, such as gated communities in Florida. "It's great!" they'd tell us. "I have six Saturdays and a Sunday every week. I never do anything!" This wasn't strictly true, of course. I knew they played golf and bridge and complained about their teeth and worried about their investment portfolios. I was certain this would not be our fate — frankly, we'd rather be smeared with honey and staked out over an anthill during our golden years — but what *did* the future hold? We were still relatively young (that wonderfully elastic phrase), but we weren't actually getting any younger. Rich and I gradually realized we were doing the same things over and over, but slightly less of them every year. Were we supposed to just soldier on for a while and then sit around waiting to crumble? What fun was that?

Then some friends invited us to visit them at their timeshare at a resort in Marbella, a town on the southern coast of Spain. Rich and I had each visited Spain long before we met, during our various youthful adventures, but neither of us had felt any particular urge to return. However, we liked the friends, and the dates happened to match up to a trip we'd already planned to Italy for the following week, so we decided to go.

We arrived at the Malaga airport to discover that by some whim of the Spanish gods, our low-budget rental car had been upgraded to a sporty convertible. As we sped along the coast road, sun-drenched and windblown and feeling pretty zippy, we were struck by how much this part of Spain resembled California: balmy air, palm trees, sparkling blue sea, all the signs and billboards in Spanish. The resemblance made us instantly feel at home; I'm a fourth-generation Californian, and Rich had been living in the Golden State for nearly twenty years when we met. When he took the job in Cleveland we created a good life for ourselves there, but now, driving along the sunny coast, I felt a deep pang of nostalgia for my native habitat.

I soon discovered that much as I loved southern Spain (or Andalucía, as it's properly called), I didn't care much for Marbella. It's situated on a part of the Spanish coast that enjoys some of the loveliest weather in the world — 320 days of full sun a year — and has endless stretches of perfect white-sand beach. These blessings had the unfortunate effect of attracting the attention of the jet set in the 1960s. As film stars and minor royalty and nouveau American millionaires began to flock in via the new airport, the city flung itself into building the sixties-style high-rise hotels and cookie-cutter tourist restaurants it felt would be worthy of its new guests. Most of the glamorous rich have long since moved down the coast to Puerto Banus, which boasts a busy yacht harbor and hundreds of jewelry shops and shoe stores frequented by very pretty young women in bikinis and high heels and not much else. Today, Marbella tends to attract Europeans taking advantage of cheap airfares and package tours. Aside from visiting the tiny, ancient Moorish section and a town square filled with peculiar Salvador Dali sculptures, there isn't much to do in Marbella beyond watching seventy-year-old British and German matrons sunbathing topless on the beach, an activity best followed by drinking heavily in the bars.

As we wandered around the town, I noticed that Rich's eyes had a tendency to light up whenever he saw a sign advertising a Spanish language course for foreigners. A few years earlier he had told me that there were two things he regretted not studying as a child: a musical instrument and a foreign language. That was when he announced he wanted to enroll in a course called "Music for Everyone" at a sort of New Age summer camp for adults in upstate New York. The course appeared to involve trying out various musical instruments and tapping your inner virtuoso.

"It says, 'No musical experience necessary,'" he read aloud from the catalog. "That's me!"

During the week of Music for Everyone, as I drifted by the music hall en route to my yoga and meditation classes, I kept hearing random bits of sound — the squiggle of a violin here, the belch of a bassoon there — accompanied by great gusts of laughter. Whatever they were doing, it sounded like they were enjoying it. At night in our cabin, Rich mentioned that most of the other students were trained musicians who were experimenting with new instruments.

"Everyone is supposed to find the one that calls to them," he explained.

"What's yours?" I asked.

"I don't know yet. So far I've eliminated the violin, oboe, piccolo, and guitar."

Every day, the list of instruments he'd eliminated grew longer and the concert at the end of the week, featuring an original work written and performed by the students, drew closer. The others were starting to work up themes and melodies, and Rich still hadn't found his instrument.

The day of the concert finally dawned, and Rich ate a hearty breakfast and strolled unconcernedly off to the music hall. I spent the day in a workshop exploring my inner being, which at the time was largely occupied with worrying about Rich's role in the upcoming performance. When it was time for the concert, I took my seat in the auditorium and looked around for Rich. I finally spotted him sitting at the very back of the little orchestra, holding an instrument I couldn't see. The other students proceeded to play a lively tune while Rich remained poised and alert, waiting for his cue. After the music swelled to its final crescendo, there was a split second of total silence as all the musicians turned to Rich. He stood up holding a triangle and struck a single, perfect note to finish off the piece. The audience and the orchestra erupted in a standing ovation.

That was pretty much it for Rich's musical career. And now he was interested in pursuing his other lifetime goal: learning a foreign language. Would his linguistic skills prove to be on a par with his ability with the violin, oboe, piccolo, and guitar?

"What do you think?" he said. "If we spend a month or six weeks in one of those intensive courses, we should be able to learn enough Spanish to get by. It could be fun."

I thought he was being a trifle overoptimistic about our ability to pick up a working knowledge of Spanish in six weeks. If you've ever studied a foreign language, especially once you were well past college age, you'll know that it requires a considerable amount of time and effort. During our travels, especially the volunteer work assignments, Rich and I had painstakingly acquired phrases in Bosnian, Georgian, Dzongkha, and various other tongues. I'd often marveled at the way each language reflects the national character. For instance, in the former Soviet republic of Georgia, the everyday greeting (*garmajoba*) and the standard toast (*garmajos*) are both taken from the word "victory," something with which the Georgians have had an extremely slim acquaintance since their heyday in the fourth century.

In Japan, we found that the rules of etiquette make it excruciatingly difficult for anyone to say no, especially to a visitor. So if you ask, say, "Does this train go to Tokyo?" they will nod and tell you it does, not wanting to disappoint you by mentioning that getting there by this particular train would entail seven transfers with layovers lasting hours, if not days. I once looked up the word for "no" in Japanese because I'd never actually heard it. I found the entry *iiya*, with this English translation: "no, nay, yes, well." Which nicely summed up the Japanese attitude. We soon learned to phrase our questions more carefully. "What is the most direct train to Tokyo?" tended to yield better results.

I once spent two weeks painting Corsica's landscapes in the company of some California artists. There I learned that the Corsican national art form is the vendetta. In that charming island country, it's not enough just to get even; you're supposed do it with originality, flair, and if possible, cutlery — the local shop windows are bristling with wicked-looking knives. When I downloaded a very brief set of Corsican phrases every traveler should know, prominent among them were *Ùn aghju fattu nunda di male* (I haven't done anything wrong), *Hè un sbagliu* (It was a misunderstanding), and *Induva mi purteti?* (Where are you taking me?). Luckily I was never in a position that required using any of these phrases. In fact, everyone I encountered was scrupulously polite; I suspect this is because you never know if the person you cut off in traffic will show up later to cut something off of you with one of those gleaming knives.

The only time my life was in danger in Corsica came one late afternoon when I was out walking alone in the country and was set upon by two large guard dogs. I'd had a frustrating day of painting and was in no mood to be trifled with, and I told them so. When the dogs kept barking and jumping around me, I shouted at them so fiercely that they froze, cowered, then ran off in fright. In fact, I am pretty sure I heard one of them say *Ùn aghju fattu nunda di male* (I haven't done anything wrong), *hè un sbagliu* (it was a misunderstanding).

I had no doubt that Spanish would involve its own linguistic adventures. We might not master it in six weeks, but I was willing to give it a shot and see how far we got.

"We could sign up for one of those intensive language courses next spring," I agreed. "But do we really want to spend a whole month in Marbella?"

"Would you rather spend February in Cleveland?" Rich countered.

He had a point. Much as we loved our home and community, there was no getting around the fact that our town, some forty-five minutes outside of the city, was in the snow belt of a region that got just sixty-nine days of full sun a year. In our neighborhood, February was cold, dark, snowy, slushy, and muddy, and it felt like the longest month of the year. I shuddered at the very thought of it.

"Let's go check out some language schools," I said.

The first school we visited was so new, the paint was barely dry. "We are good school," the overeager staff assured us. "You happy here." Like most people we'd met in Marbella's touristy downtown, they spoke enough English to make themselves understood. They then proceeded to do everything short of handcuffing us to the railings in an effort to convince us to stay on as paying customers. The second school had a considerably longer track record, but it was upstairs from both a sex shop and a pet store. We didn't mind the sex shop but felt we couldn't really concentrate in an atmosphere thick with the odor of kitty litter and molting parrots. The third school had been around for thirty years and didn't smell of anything in particular.

We signed up, little realizing our lives were about to change forever.

Chapter 2

LEARNING THE LANGUAGE

꿏

Rich and I arrived five minutes late for our first Spanish class and spent the next five years trying to catch up.

Our fellow students were mostly twenty-something Europeans who already spoke half a dozen languages and found Spanish almost laughably easy to acquire. They were in Spain taking advantage of a European Union program that provided a month of free classes followed by a month or two working as an unpaid intern for a local company. The program was meant to help unite the disparate elements of the EU, forging new bonds of friendship and cultural exchange. It worked perfectly, although possibly not precisely as the designers intended. The twenty-somethings showed up at the school for a few hours every day, then passed the rest of their time sunbathing on the beach or displaying their cool and their tans in various nightclubs, drinking cheap beer and flirting with the locals. From what I could tell, a considerable amount of late-night conjugating was taking place. If and when the students showed up for class, their agile young brains, even with the impediments of a hangover and lack of sleep, ran circles around ours. It was extremely annoying, especially when coupled with a patronizing attitude toward the old slowpokes.

Meanwhile I was setting the alarm earlier and earlier every morning, huddling under the covers with cups of tea and stacks of books and homework papers as I attempted to make sense of the complexities of Spanish verbs.

"Do you realize Spanish verbs come in" — I counted them up — "fourteen tenses, plus a gerund and a past participle?"

"What's a gerund?" asked Rich, whose early English grammar classes had not been quite as rigorous as those I'd attended at the Convent of the Sacred Heart.

But I didn't hear him, because I was frowning at another part of the page. "And according to this, the imperative isn't a tense, it's something called a mood." I felt it was highly unfair that the verbs were allowed to have moods, while I was expected to remain cheerful and alert throughout a day spent in the company of condescending kids.

Our teachers patiently put us through various exercises, such as showing us flash cards with scenes of daily life. While our fellow *alumnos* (students) all seemed to have hundreds of vocabulary words on tap, Rich and I were still struggling to distinguish *pollo* (chicken) from *pelo* (hair) and *perro* (dog). A typical exchange would go like this:

Teacher, holding up a picture: "*¿Que hace ella?*" (What is she doing?)

Me, after a long pause: "*¿Cepilla su pollo?*" (Brushing her chicken?)

Rich, after a longer pause: "*¿Camina su pelo?*" (Walking her hair?)

At the end of five days of this mutual torture, everyone was greatly relieved to break for the weekend. Rich and I used the time to go exploring, and one weekend when some American friends came to visit us, we all decided to take a road trip to Seville. Here we found an enchanting city with roots that go a lot deeper than Marbella's. It's common knowledge among the citizenry that Seville was founded by Hercules — yes, that Hercules, the demigod son of Zeus (or Jupiter, if you happen to be Roman rather than Greek). Over the next two thousand years, the city was shaped by a Who's Who of ancient civilizations, including the Phoenicians, the Romans, the Visigoths, and the Moors, until 1248, when King Ferdinand III retook the city in the name of Christian Spain and got himself canonized for his efforts.

Then in 1492, Isabella and her Ferdinand chose the city to stage the sendoff of Christopher Columbus. In one of its rare shrewd business moves, Seville somehow parlayed this into a contract to receive *everything* Columbus and all future expeditions would bring back to Europe from the New World. Overnight the city became rich beyond its wildest dreams, and Sevillanos spent the next 150 years happily commissioning lavish palaces, churches, convents, and works of public and private art in the exuberant styles of the day.

Eventually, due to the usual mix of corruption, infighting, and sloth, Seville lost the contract, and without New World treasures pouring in, the city soon sank back down to its former status of economic backwater. While the locals naturally view this as the worst sort of luck, the rest of us are delighted with the results. Twenty-first-century Seville is an affordable, peaceful, and safe city, with lively street life at all hours of the day and night, set against a backdrop of magnificent old buildings. While urban sprawl and sixties-style monstrosities blight the outskirts, as they do everywhere in these architecturally challenged times, the heart of Seville retains much of its ancient charm. Confined on three sides by a sweeping curve of the Guadalquivir River, the central city remains comfortably small, an area you can walk across in half an hour.

I say you *can* walk across the city in half an hour — I've done it myself, countless times — but the chances of your doing this on your first visit are astronomically small. One of the first things you discover upon arrival is that the city's layout is byzantine in its complexity, with narrow, cobbled streets winding charmingly, but maddeningly, in every direction but the one you want to go. The next thing you'll learn is that all the city maps are wrong. Over the years I've consulted dozens of maps created by the tourist bureau, the major department store, various hotels, and a host of bars eager for my business. Every one of them contains wild inaccuracies about the size, relative position, and even existence of various streets — such as the little alleyway we live on, which is often overlooked entirely. The maps are not completely useless, but it's best to approach them the way you would a route that your Uncle Louie sketched on the back of a napkin while sitting in a pub: better than nothing, but certainly not up to GPS standards of accuracy.

My theory is that local mapmakers feel they wouldn't be doing their job if they didn't help you along with a few hints to give you a richer and more nuanced understanding of the city's geography. For instance, if there is a useful little alley linking two busy streets, they'll make sure you don't overlook it by drawing it three times its actual size. This often leaves more literal-minded visitors seeking a major thoroughfare when in fact, the alleged street is a pedestrian alley so narrow you can't get down it with your umbrella up. None of the maps include a compass mark indicating true north, because it's plainly irrelevant. In this serpentine city, people orient themselves by plazas and landmarks; like spaceships, they rely on the gravitational force of these larger bodies to draw them in, swing them around, and shoot them off in the next direction they want to go. Ask locals how to get somewhere, and they'll explain how to find the next plaza and tell you to inquire again from there.

Of course, I knew nothing of this when I first set foot in Seville. I arrived in happy confidence that Rich's legendary orienteering skills, which had enabled him to grasp the complexities of cities such as Istanbul in five minutes of skimming a map, would be more than equal to the task. I was so wrong. Like most visitors, we managed to make our way to the city's center point, the world's largest gothic cathedral, with its 344-foot tower known as the Giralda. We strolled off down a side street and were soon hopelessly lost in the labyrinthine streets of Santa Cruz, a barrio built to house the Jews during the five hundred years of Moorish rule. Like all first-time visitors, we spent the next hours fetching up on street corners clutching our map, muttering in bewilderment, "But it says right here..."

The local guidebooks attempt to pass this off as an advantage, saying blithely, "Allow some time for losing yourself in the quaint back streets of the city, where you'll discover the real Seville." This is true, in its way. The real Seville isn't the magnificent sixteenth-century buildings listed in our guidebook, but rather the convivial groups of locals clustered in cafés and tapas bars, drinking beer and nibbling on olives and ham, chatting vivaciously and smoking one cigarette after another. They all looked like they were having a terrific time, and we wished we knew enough Spanish to join in the fun. Unfortunately, our language skills weren't even adequate for asking directions.

So with nothing more reliable than an idiosyncratic tourist map to guide our steps, Rich and I kept wandering through the narrow city streets, hoping to find a landmark that we could steer by to make the return journey to our hotel. Finding ourselves outside a charming old *palacio* with a tiled courtyard, we noticed a small plaque on its wall announcing that it was a language school, and we wandered in to take a look around. The courtyard was full of sunlight and small groups of students laboriously conversing in rudimentary Spanish. The small library was well stocked with textbooks, audiotapes, and several shelves of novels in Spanish and English. The staff was welcoming, the curriculum looked interesting, and the price was right. We immediately decided that the following year we would return to Seville to continue our Spanish studies.

Upon arriving the next spring, we showed up at the school for orientation and were given a short written test to identify our level of Spanish. When I brought my completed test to the front desk, the woman sitting there looked up at me and said something that sounded like this:

"*Cuandoempieceelcurso   tienesqueelegir   tusasignaturas duranteelprimerdiádeclase.   Antesdematricularte   enlasecretaría tucoordinador tienequevery firmarlalistacon lasasignaturas.*"

I stared at her blankly. Was she even speaking Spanish? Seeing my confusion, she kindly repeated the whole thing a little more slowly. It didn't help one bit. For the first time, I felt a stab of anxiety. Class hadn't even started yet, and I seemed to be failing. What had I gotten myself into?

Another approach was clearly in order. I knew and respected the school policy that decreed nothing but Spanish was to be spoken in the classroom, but perhaps on the first day she would cut me a little slack during the administrative process.

"*No entiendo,*" I said. (I don't understand.) That much Spanish I knew for sure. I added in my own language, "May I speak English for a moment?"

She shrugged and said distinctly, "*Pero no hablo inglés.*" (But I don't speak English.) "*Ni una palabra.*" (Not one word.)

I was stunned. It had simply never occurred to me that people in the business of teaching Spanish to foreigners, including a large number of Americans, would not have learned the most universal language of our times. The people I'd worked with in Bosnia and the republic of Georgia had all spoken English, for heaven's sake, as did everyone in Marbella who came in contact with foreigners. What was going on here?

This was my first inkling of just how different Seville would prove to be. Civilized, yes. Americanized, not so much.

Rich came up beside me, clutching his paperwork. "What do we do now?" he asked me.

"I'm not sure. I seem to be flying without a net here."

We somehow stumbled through an entire day of incomprehensible orientation procedures, at the end of which we had learned little beyond the number of the classroom at which we were to present ourselves the following morning.

There, we soon discovered that while this language school was much larger, lovelier, and more dynamic than the one we'd attended in Marbella, our time was still spent drilling in grammar and making awkward conversation with other beginners. Our fellow *alumnos* were once again young, multilingual Europeans who seemed entirely unmoved by such shocking revelations as the fact that there are two different words for "for" and two different verbs that mean "to be." (Could this have been what Bill Clinton meant when he so famously said, "It depends on what your definition of 'is' is"?) Using the wrong version of "to be" can radically alter the meaning of a phrase. Broadly speaking, the verb *ser* is used for permanent states, such as your nationality, and the verb *estar* for conditions that may change, such as your state of health. For instance, you would use the *ser* form to say "*Es Rodríguez*," meaning "He is Rodríguez" or "His last name is Rodríguez." However, because the name Rodríguez is as common in Spain as Smith is in the US, in Andalucía it has given rise to another phrase using *estar*. To say that someone "*está de Rodríguez*" means "He is temporarily Rodríguez" or "His wife's away and he is going by a false name so he can go out and have a little illicit fun."

It took me a while to realize that our formal lessons were only a prequel to the real work of learning the language: using it in daily life. Speaking Spanish in the classroom was akin to reading the owner's manual of a car and playing arcade games that involve a steering wheel. Those can be helpful preliminaries, but at some point you have to start test-driving on real roads. One of the great (and at times frustrating and/or terrifying) things about Seville is that you have endless opportunities to practice your language skills, because almost nobody in the city speaks English. If you want to eat, drink, find the bathroom, or buy laundry detergent, sooner or later you're going to have to come up with the appropriate vocabulary.

Those who try to avoid test-driving their new language have a rough time of it. "I'm not going to speak any Spanish outside the classroom until I am fluent," announced a young British friend who was planning to live in Seville indefinitely. A few months later, he gave up and went back to England, frustrated because he didn't feel he fit in. What a surprise!

At our school, class began at nine o'clock with grammar lessons, in which we grappled with irregular verbs, the structure of interrogatives, and other linguistic complexities. At quarter to eleven we were released for the midmorning break, and we'd all rush out to the nearest bar for a second breakfast. This fine Sevillano tradition consists of small baguettes sliced in half, toasted, and dripping with olive oil, topped with ham, chopped tomatoes, or sugar, accompanied by a cup of coffee. Long before Starbucks made ordering caffeinated beverages as complex as the preflight check of an air-to-air combat plane, the Sevillanos organized their coffee into subtly calibrated categories, which naturally figured large in our early vocabulary acquisition. There was *café con leche* (a small glass filled half with espresso, half with milk), *café solo* (a straight shot of espresso, and quite an eye-opener), *leche manchada* (literally "stained milk," a half inch of espresso in the bottom of a glass of steamed milk), *café americano* (very weak coffee served in a cup and saucer), *descafeinado* (instant powdered decaf), and *descafeinado de máquina* (decaf espresso made in an espresso machine from fresh grounds, which of course could be ordered in any of the above configurations).

Tea drinkers had an easier time of it, unless (like me) they wanted a cup of tea with a little milk. Although that's not a terribly unusual beverage in Seville, ordering it is generally greeted with disbelief and incomprehension. If you say *té con leche* (tea with milk), they give you a tea bag stuck in a cup of boiled milk, which is horrid. If you say *té con leche aparte* (tea with milk apart, or on the side), they bring you tea, but not the milk. Apparently by "apart," they assume you mean in another room, or on someone else's table. To be as clear as possible, I usually specify *té hecho con agua, con un poco de leche aparte para añadir* (tea made with water, with a little milk on the side to add in), which may work out in the end, although I generally have to send back the tea-bag-in-milk version once or twice before getting what I've asked for. You can see how invaluable this kind of experience is to the language student seeking to expand her vocabulary.

I became proficient in yet more vital terminology as I picked up various social customs associated with the Spanish café/bar scene, such as paying and tipping. One of the first things you learn is that you never pay up front. The barman keeps track of *la cuenta* (your tab) in his head or by writing it in chalk on top of the bar, although some places are now finding it more convenient, if less quaint, to install computers. When settling the tab, Sevillanos rarely leave a *propina* (tip). If anything, they might leave behind a few small coins from the change they get back after paying the bill. Tipping is simply not the custom, since service is included in the price and waiters are a professional class whose salaries are supposed to provide a living wage. Except in places catering mainly to foreign tourists, a customer leaving behind an extra 15 or 20 percent of the bill would be viewed as peculiar and inappropriate, as if you'd insisted on paying an additional twenty euros for a sweater in a shop.

Even without having to calculate a *propina*, paying my bar bill at the end of the midmorning break was a tricky business in a bar that was *lleno de gente* (full of people) who were just finishing up their second breakfast. First I had to flag down the barman, then I had to recall enough vocabulary to remind him what I'd ordered, and then — if it wasn't written on the surface of the bar where I could read it upside down — I had to attempt to understand the numbers he was shouting over the din. The whole process could take longer than consuming my tea and toast.

Arriving back at the school, we'd usually begin the second half of class with conversation, which, given our lack of fluency, was pretty limited. The teacher would start us off by asking, say, about our impressions of Seville.

"*Es una ciudad bonita*," one of the European youths would toss out. (It's a beautiful city.)

"*Mucho bonita*," I would add. (A lot beautiful.)

"*Sevilla*," Rich would chime in, catching the ball but not exactly running with it.

When this became too excruciatingly dull, the teacher would have us read aloud from the newspaper while she half dozed at her desk, rousing herself occasionally to correct our pronunciation or give us another article to read.

In our off hours, Rich and I roamed the city, gradually becoming familiar with the major plazas and landmarks that the locals use in navigating the neighborhoods. We'd often stop for tapas at one of Seville's three thousand bars, attempting to decipher the menus that were scrawled on blackboards nailed to the walls. Few of the offerings appeared in our dictionary, and some that we thought we recognized actually turned out to be something else entirely, a phenomenon our dictionary likes to call a "false amigo." For instance, you can imagine our surprise when the tortilla, familiar to every Californian as the thin, bread-like outer layer of tacos and burritos, turned out to be a sort of dense omelet, most commonly made with potatoes and onions. We memorized a few favorites, such as *boquerones* (anchovies marinated in wine vinegar) and *espinacas con garbanzos* (spinach with chickpeas and cumin), and took to frequenting places that displayed their offerings in glass cases, where we could point to whatever looked the most appetizing.

Dining out in the city's tapas bars served to enrich our fledgling vocabulary, and in those early days we were pathetically grateful for anything that would boost our learning curve. Rich was struggling even more than I was, largely because I had the advantage of having studied French as a child under the Paris-based nuns of the Sacred Heart. This helped me face up more easily to certain unwelcome realities, such as that every noun has a gender and you have to learn it. Also, having worked as a journalist, I was more thoroughly grounded in English grammar, which helped me distinguish an adverb from an adjective and, on a good day, a gerund from a past participle. I'd been trained to be a stickler about punctuation, and it was with something like astonishment that I learned how differently the Spanish approach the matter. For instance, they set off dialogue with dashes, not quotation marks, and clue you in that an interrogative is imminent by putting an inverted question mark at the beginning of the sentence as well as the standard one at the end. ¿Why don't *we* do that? Similarly, when an exciting phrase is about to jump out at you, they give you a head's up with a dash and then throw in an upside down exclamation point right there — ¡in the middle of the sentence!

Listening to Spanish was far more of a challenge than deciphering it on the printed page. Part of the difficulty lay in the molasses-thick regional accent of Andalucía; it was like studying English in rural Mississippi. The Andalucíans love to talk — at length, at speed, at high volume, and at the same time as everyone else in the room. In their eagerness to get their point across more quickly, they have developed the habit of dropping bits of words, usually their endings. This can be disconcerting to the uninitiated, because the endings tell you the gender and number of nouns and the tense or mood of the verb, information that is generally considered useful, if not downright vital, to the listener. Even the simple greeting *buenos días* (good day) is shortened to *buen di* or simply *buenos,* as if to say, "Oh, you know what I mean. Do I *really* need to spell it out for you?"

Our greatest challenge in the early years was an old man named Antonio, who had an impenetrable Andalucían accent and a tendency to mumble that was compounded by the loss of several important front teeth. He ran a tiny neighborhood bar where he sold beer and wine for eighty-five céntimos (then about a dollar) per glass. Antonio became our benchmark; we told ourselves that if the day ever dawned when we could understand him, we could truly say we spoke Andalucían — or as they call it, Andalú. Rich and I used to hang out in Antonio's bar, sipping small glasses of beer and wine, looking at the walls crowded with plastic models of military planes, photos of bullfighters cut out of the newspaper, and in the place of honor behind the bar, a black-draped portrait of Franco (whose face is about as popular in Seville as Hitler's is in the rest of Europe). The first time we were there, Rich left a twenty-cent tip on the bar. Antonio glowered at it for a moment before pushing it back across the scarred wooden surface. "This isn't that kind of bar," he growled. At least, we think that's what he said. It might have been, "Thanks for killing the bear," or something even less likely. We'll never know, since sadly, Antonio's place closed before we mastered enough Andalú to be certain we were catching his drift.

Another early hangout was a tiny bar around the corner from our apartment, whose owner, Vicente, used to sing in a beautiful tenor voice at midnight on Saturday nights. Singing or speaking, Vicente was easier to understand than Antonio, being in possession of nearly all his teeth, but he spoke very quickly with a heavy Andalú accent, and we often struggled to make sense of what he was telling us.

One night as we headed over to Vicente's, Rich said to me, "Look, I know I sometimes ask for help if I get stuck, but I think it's time I floundered ahead on my own. From now on, I want you to stop jumping in. Whatever is going on, I will figure it out and handle it in my own way."

"Fine," I said. "My lips are zipped."

As soon as we walked in, Vicente hurried over to kiss my hand and usher us to one of the three little wooden tables at the back, talking rapidly all the while about the dishes he'd cooked up for that evening.

"Don't you think we ought to stop and look at the food in the display case, to see what we want to eat?" I whispered to Rich.

"No," he said firmly. "I will handle this."

Lips firmly zipped, I listened to the flood of words coming from Vicente and managed to grasp that he was suggesting a nice green salad for me and, for Rich, a big bowl of *menudo* (tripe stew), a dish he particularly loathes.

"Yes, yes, that will be fine," Rich told Vicente grandly.

When the tripe stew appeared in front of Rich, he paled. "What's this?" he said to me.

"The *menudo* you ordered."

"I can't eat this!"

I shrugged and dug into my salad while he pushed the stew around in the bowl with his fork. "Seriously," he said. "I can't eat it."

"Look, why don't you just tell Vicente that it's delicious, but you're just not very hungry tonight."

Vicente came by a few minutes later, looked at the untouched *menudo*, and asked if everything was all right.

Now at this point, what Rich meant to say was "*No tengo hambre*," literally "I don't have hunger," meaning "I'm not hungry." But what he actually said was *"No tengo hombre,"* which means "I don't have a man."

"*¿Qué?*" said Vicente. (Say what?)

"*¡No tengo hombre!*" Rich repeated more loudly. (I don't have a man!)

Vicente looked confused, then nervous. He backed away from the table and left us strictly alone for the rest of the evening.

Rich, of course, has never lived this down, and it was months before we could bring ourselves to face Vicente again.

Meanwhile, back at the language school, we were attempting to use the present tense, the future tense, and something called the *preterito perfecto*, which they claim we have in English as well, although I'd never heard of it. We were struggling with using auxiliary verbs to make compound tenses, and there were rumors of worse to come. Advanced students spoke with fear and loathing of a verb form called the *subjuntivo*. Peeking ahead in my verb book, I read that the *subjuntivo* was used to express, among other things, a wish, insistence, preference, suggestion, request, doubt, fear, joy, hope, sorrow, necessity, regret, importance, urgency, or possibility; it should appear after certain conjunctions indicating time and in adjectival clauses if the antecedent is something or someone that is indefinite, negative, vague, or nonexistent. Head spinning, I read on until I reached the section on the past or imperfect *subjuntivo*, which said helpfully, "However, if the verb in the main clause is in the imperfect indicative, preterit, conditional, or pluperfect indicative, the imperfect subjunctive (this form) or pluperfect subjunctive is ordinarily used in the dependent clause — provided, of course, that there is some element that requires the use of the subjunctive." At which point I threw the book down and went out for a walk.

So it was only later that the final blow fell, and I discovered that the past tense known as the imperfect subjunctive comes in two forms, which can be used interchangeably, and you have to learn both of them. I mean really, who authorized that bit of nonsense? Can't we all just agree to use either *estudiara* or *estudiase* when we want to talk about wishing we had studied harder?

At that point, the *subjuntivo* was just a storm cloud on the far horizon; I was still struggling to compose sentences that went past the "see Spot run" level. Rich was lagging even further behind, increasingly frustrated by the challenges of learning a complex subject at the rapid pace set by kids just out of college, at the peak of their learning abilities, who had little patience for anyone who couldn't keep up.

Clearly the whole language-acquisition process was going to take more time than we thought. We decided to come back for a second spring vacation in Seville to get a little more Spanish under out belt. This time around we opted for afternoon classes, and I took to buying Rich a coffee on the way to class to get his synapses firing. Some days it was a beer to shore up his courage. Then Rich had the bright idea of switching to private lessons. He sat down with his teacher, a pleasant young woman who wanted to keep her job, and explained that from now on he would not be taking any tests or getting grades, he would do only those homework assignments he chose, and he was not going to put up with being chastised if he got back three minutes late from the break. Things got much better after that.

I decided Rich had the right idea, and by our third spring in Seville we were both taking private lessons with a teacher named Yolanda, a tiny, vivacious woman who vibrated with so much energy she seemed to extract better Spanish from us by sheer willpower. Often our lessons were long walks through the city's back streets, dropping in on tiny shops, tapas bars, and artisan workshops we happened to pass. "*Es Sevilla profunda,*" she'd say of the place — this is the "profound," or real, Seville. We'd do our best to engage in conversation with the various proprietors, often resorting to hand signals to support our rudimentary Spanish. I never thought I'd be so grateful for my family's penchant for playing charades.

With Yolanda's help, Rich and I began making better progress. And I figured out a few labor-saving tricks for meeting daily challenges, such as always ordering a quarter of a kilo of whatever groceries I wanted in the markets. It was all I could do to remember the names of each of the vegetables, fruits, herbs, fish, and cheeses without getting further tangled up with the numbers and the metric system as well. After a while I did learn the numbers, and I actually grew quite fond of the metric system, which defines my weight as fifty-four and my bra size as ninety-five.

We got yet more Spanish practice every Friday when the landlady came around. During our spring vacations, we rented a small, charming apartment above a bread store in a busy neighborhood near the cathedral. We paid the weekly rent in cash to our landlady, Luz, a pretty blonde about my own age with an abundance of tawny faux fur and glittery jewelry, a shrewd business sense, and an irrepressible twinkle in her eye. Because she was used to dealing with foreigners, she spoke slowly and loudly, as if we were incapacitated or drunk. "BUENOS DÍAS," she'd enunciate. "¿CÓMO ESTÁIS?" (HOW ARE YOU?) We would reply in our halting Spanish, and as she counted the rent money, she would ask us about our studies and our experiences in the city. She appeared to get a tremendous kick out of our enthusiasm, and pretty soon we were meeting her at the café downstairs for drinks. After that it was just a short step to the first of many cultural excursions and rounds of beer with Luz and her husband, Toño.

So Rich and I were learning the language (yes we were!) and making friends. Every day we discovered something new about the city and its culture. Every night we checked out another tapas bar or flamenco show or concert. Every year, it got harder to leave Seville and fly back to the snowy, gray skies of Ohio.

During our fourth spring vacation, Rich sat me down at a sidewalk café table and out of nowhere suggested that we spend a year in Seville.

"It would be a sort of sabbatical," he said. "We could really immerse ourselves in the language and finally get our arms around it properly." I started to speak, but he held up his hand as if to still my protests. "Just one year. It would be a sort of extended vacation, really. Not a life-changing move. Of course we aren't going to sell our house or anything crazy like that. We'll just stretch our yearly trip from three months to twelve. Hey, we've been back three times, plus one for good measure. We know we could live here. I think a year—"

"Yes!"

"You don't have to decide right away... Wait, did you say 'yes'?"

"Absolutely. I'm in." In? I was thrilled. After all this time, we were finally going to live abroad for a year! It was a heady thought for both of us, and it took us quite a while to come down to earth enough to start thinking about the practical aspects.

The first hurdle, we knew, would be getting a long-term visa, one that would be good for a year instead of the ninety days allowed for a standard tourist visit. To find out how to go about it, we decided to consult the highest-ranking American official in Seville, the United States consular agent. He turned out to be an unsympathetic old character with a gnarled face and a crusty attitude; glowering at us, he muttered that we should deal with this through a Spanish embassy in the US. With that, he turned and stomped away, leaving us with the distinct impression that the last thing he wanted was more Americans cluttering up his town. Somehow I had expected a professional diplomat to be more... well, diplomatic.

He may have been less than *simpático,* but the consular agent was correct. As soon as we got back to Ohio, we contacted the nearest Spanish consulate, which was in Chicago. They informed us that obtaining a one-year residency visa was simple. All we had to do was fill out a packet of forms and attach such documents as proof of health insurance, bank statements, highlights of our investment portfolio, details of Rich's pension, a statement of our upcoming Social Security benefits, a letter from our police chief confirming that we weren't wanted by any federal, state, county, or township law enforcement agencies, and a note from our doctor saying we were healthy enough to survive in a country where everyone lived on cigarettes, ham, and coffee. What, no epistle from the priest about how long it had been since our last confession?

It took us until August to assemble the information, at which point the Spanish consulate informed us we had to bring them the packet ourselves. Apparently they only placed so much confidence in the written word and felt that a personal sizing-up was required. We turned over the thick stack of documents with complete (and, as it turned out, entirely misplaced) confidence that having done everything they asked, all we had to do now was sit back and wait for our visas to be granted.

And when I say sit back, I really mean we sprang into action on another front.

In October, we flew to Seville to start house hunting, or as five years of language lessons enabled us to say, *para buscar una casa.*

Chapter 3

HOUSE HUNTING

❧

"We have three main criteria," I told the rental agent in Seville. "We need a terrace, so Rich can grow his plants. We want to be near the river or a park, because we're bringing our dog over. And we absolutely do not want to live in the area around Plaza Alfalfa, because of the *botellones*." These were the impromptu outdoor drinking parties in which young Sevillanos gathered to share bottles (hence the name) of various alcoholic beverages. *Botellones* sprang up all over the city, especially on weekend nights, and often lasted until dawn. Among the largest were the ones crowding the Alfalfa neighborhood's narrow side streets, and — call me crazy — I didn't care much for the idea of having five or six hundred drunken youths partying on my doorstep night after night until dawn.

Eliminating a single barrio wasn't a problem, since Seville is blessed with dozens of great neighborhoods, and we checked out every one of them. Rich was in his glory, consulting newspaper ads and rental agencies, comparing features and prices, dragging me out to study the exteriors of unsuitable but interesting properties "just to get a feel for what's available." It was only the second time in our marriage that we were actually in the market for a new home, and Rich was wallowing in the opportunity to indulge his passion for real estate.

One thing we knew for certain: our new place in Seville would be nothing like the last piece of real estate we'd acquired, our country house near Cleveland.

As you may have heard, Cleveland is *not* a destination city. Unlike, say, San Francisco or Seville, people don't flock there in order to follow their bliss. In fact, various events, such as the polluted river catching fire and, in an apparently unrelated incident, the city's mayor catching his own hair on fire during a public ceremony, rendered Cleveland the butt of jokes for decades. My sisters and most of our friends were aghast when we mentioned that a headhunter had approached Rich about a position there. They couldn't believe we would seriously consider such a move.

However, despite its reputation, I was more than willing to give Cleveland a try. For one thing, I was still in the starry-eyed romantic phase and would have followed Rich to the ends of the earth (as I was later to do, in fact). For another, I happened to have heard lots of positive things about Cleveland from a former neighbor who'd grown up there. "It has a world-class art museum and the most-recorded orchestra in the world," the neighbor had told me proudly. "The suburbs are wonderful communities. It's a great place to live."

When Rich began to get serious about the Cleveland job, I went to the public library to do a little research. It took a while to locate an Ohio guidebook, and the first line I read, "Cleveland isn't all smokestacks and slag heaps," was perhaps not as reassuring as the author had intended it to be.

There was one thing the guidebook, my former neighbor, and my sisters all agreed on: Cleveland had some of the best real estate values in the country. It's the sort of place where for the price of a small studio apartment in an unfashionable part of San Francisco, you can buy a McMansion in a good neighborhood and have change left over. My only worry was that Rich wouldn't be able to stop checking out the great housing deals, and we'd spend the entire three years of his contract looking at one bargain after another, unable to make up our minds among all the tempting options.

But as it turned out, we found our Ohio home almost at once, in a semirural township called Russell that was so small our mailing address was in the next village, Chagrin Falls. The house had been built as a one-room hunting lodge (a sort of stone shack, really) back in the 1920s and had grown through the years into a rambling three-bedroom house. The rooms weren't large, but there were plenty of them, often in unexpected places. There was a big front lawn and a wide back deck that looked out over the Chagrin River and woods that were full of rabbits, deer, and raccoons. As to the price, the one our real estate agent quoted sounded suspiciously low, and then we learned she'd made a mistake and it was actually ten thousand dollars less than that.

The next day we signed the papers, and that night we lay sleepless in the hotel bed. Had we been hasty? Rich kept saying, "I didn't even ask about the septic system." I was too busy worrying about whether there were any closets — why hadn't I seen any? surely there had to be *some*? — to be bothered asking what a septic system is.

We returned to California to make arrangements with the movers and bid farewell to our family and friends in a round of dinners that left us bloated and breathless by the time we boarded the train that would take us east. "Have a great time in Cleveland," everyone said, trying not to sound too sardonic.

"Seriously, good luck. I'm sure it will be..." And here they would grope for a word that wouldn't choke them. "It'll be real."

And it was. Cleveland might not have been glamorous, but after the kaleidoscopic whirl of San Francisco, I found it oddly comforting to be in a place that was so rooted in tradition. People didn't just live there, they were *from* there, and had been for generations. Our new home was in a county that still had a large number of working farms, most of them run by Amish families. People cared about the land and about their neighbors. I realized I had better put aside my recipes for Thai chili wraps and learn to make casseroles. I called L.L.Bean and had them start sending me catalogs.

Moving into our new home, we were gratified to discover that we did have both closets and a septic system (which turned out to be a private waste-disposal system involving a holding tank and long drip lines under the lawn; who knew?). Rich soon bought a farm-sized tractor and spent many happy hours cutting the grass and hauling dirt and rocks from one part of the property to another.

One of his first projects was putting in a large vegetable garden, which would eventually supply half the neighborhood with fresh zucchini, corn, tomatoes, and herbs every summer. This was the opening salvo in a twenty-year battle with the local wildlife; the deer, raccoons, squirrels, and other varmints were determined to take more than their fair share of the bounty, and Rich was equally determined to stop them. After trying and discarding everything from special netting to an ultrasonic system, Rich discovered a solar-powered electric "wildlife solution" on the Internet.

"It's sort of like the Invisible Fence for dogs," he explained. "You train the animals not to go near the area."

"I'm game," I said, "but how are you going to get the deer to wear the collars?"

"You don't. You lure them over to the fence by hanging foil-lined peanut butter cups all over it. I guess just about all animals like the smell. When they nuzzle the cups, they get zapped. Pretty soon they change their traffic patterns and leave our garden alone."

The first night we turned the fence on, I was sure we'd wake up in the morning to find deer carcasses scattered around the perimeter of the garden, or possibly the scorched bodies of neighborhood children or dogs. But we soon learned that having fifteen volts of electricity shooting through your body doesn't do any actual damage. It is, however, a hideous sensation, and one with which I was to become all too familiar, since we often forgot whether the fence was on or off during busy seasons in the garden. It's not pain, exactly, it's every cell in your body suddenly shrieking, "WHAT THE HELL? DO *not* DO THAT AGAIN!"

The electric fence was highly successful, repelling not only deer but smaller animals that got shocked to their toes when trying to climb over the wire. It also attracted every kid in the neighborhood, and it became something of a rite of passage to "accidentally" touch the electric fence and get zapped with their friends looking on. Posting a dramatic yellow sign covered with lightning bolts and dire warnings only served to encourage them.

One day some neighbors stopped in with their houseguests, and as we all stood around chatting, one of the houseguests noticed that our dog had accidentally been shut inside the garden when we closed the gate. The young man kindly reached through the fence to pet the dog, and just as his hand came in contact with her head, his chin touched the electric wire. Dog and man flew apart with identical howls of shocked surprise.

I rushed over to apologize, explaining this was an electric fence to keep out pests. "Well, it works," he said shortly. "You won't see *me* around your garden again."

Nor did we. But we were not lacking in other company. Squirrels and bats paid us visits, slipping into our ground-floor bedroom from the screened porch and causing pandemonium until they were chased out. Moles occasionally wandered through the kitchen. The attic was alive with mice, despite the energetic efforts of the local exterminator, who kept placing bright blue poison pellets around the attic floor in the cherished but mistaken belief that it would reduce the mouse population to a manageable level.

One morning I was in my home office, frantically typing away on a report I needed to take with me on a business trip that very afternoon. I was deep into the final stages of a long, complex appendix when Rich burst into my office. Without taking my eyes off the screen I said, "I don't care if the house is on fire. I have to finish this report."

"Okay," he said. "I just thought you might want to know there's a six-foot snake on our bed."

"*What?*" I hit the "save" button and started to rise. Then my head swiveled back to the screen, which was now displaying a message telling me that the file I'd been working on since dawn had suddenly become so permanently corrupted that I couldn't even revert to the last-saved version.

I began to hyperventilate. Okay, I thought. Calm down. First things first. Let's have a look at this snake.

I followed Rich to the bedroom. There, lounging across our comforter, was a six-foot black snake, slender but with two mouse-sized bulges that suggested it was now enjoying a post-breakfast siesta. *On our bed.*

Right away I sprang into action. I grabbed the camera and took a picture. Since there are practically no snakes in Ohio, I knew no one would ever believe us without proof.

The snake seemed to find the flash annoying. While Rich and I were momentarily dithering, trying to hit on a course of action, it slithered off the comforter and went underneath the bed.

This was bad.

Now in those days, our bed was a Japanese-style futon laid on top of a lightweight wooden frame, so Rich grabbed a flashlight and very, very carefully lifted up one corner of the bed.

No snake. This was worse.

We were due to leave for the airport in three hours. I pictured myself leaving a note for the house sitter: "The dog gets two scoops of the new dog food every night, and by the way, there's a large snake loose in the house. See you Sunday."

Rich finally found the snake stretched out in the baseboard heater, trying to blend in and look like just another part of the heating element. Only its eyes moved, darting back and forth as if it were trying to figure out whether we were buying its disguise.

Now, you may think we were total wimps, but at this point we called for backup. There was a game warden on the town payroll whose sole job was to help residents deal with wild animals that had strayed into places they didn't belong, such as skunks in dog pens and deer in swimming pools and snapping turtles out on the highway. Unfortunately, the game warden wasn't available, so emergency dispatch sent over one of the local cops.

He arrived in uniform with a gun on his hip, and we took him back to see the perpetrator. Squatting down, he stared into our baseboard heater for a while and then said, "Yep, that's a snake all right."

Okay, thanks for the professional opinion. "Any idea how to get it out?" I asked.

"Got a coat hanger?" he asked.

"What do you have in mind?"

"It's like this," he said. "I stick the curved part into the heater here, hook it around the snake and kind of" — he made a sharp, yanking motion with his hand — "jerk it out through the opening here."

We all looked at the one-inch opening of the heating unit.

"I see," I said slowly. "That's a good plan, I guess, but isn't the snake's body going to get torn up all over the inside of my baseboard heater?"

We all looked at the narrow opening again. "Might," the cop admitted.

"And Plan B would be...?"

He scratched his head. "Well, we could loosen the cover of the heater, and your husband could pull it off and I could kind of grab the snake and throw it outside."

The first part sounded okay, but he lost me at "throw it outside." The snake had already found a way in once; we didn't want it taking regular naps on our futon. Could we perhaps drop it off in the woods somewhere, say at that park a few miles up the main road? The cop couldn't see any reason why not, so I went to hunt up an old pillowcase we could use to hold the captured beast.

Slowly, Rich pried up one edge of the heater cover, and the cop lunged for the snake. Fortunately, he got it. Unfortunately, he got it by the tail. The snake went wild, flailing around the room at the full extent of its body, trying to bite everybody at once. The cop hung on grimly, Rich ran around trying to get the pillowcase over the snake's head, and I kept snapping pictures. The two men finally managed to stuff the snake into the pillowcase; instantly our captive gave up the fight and went limp. Rich took a firm grip to close off the opening, and the cop dusted off his hands, wished us luck, and left us, quite literally, holding the bag.

"Let's go," Rich said. "You're driving."

He settled into the passenger seat with the pillowcase on the floor between his feet. As I drove up the highway, he said, "You know, this thing's beginning to move around a little." He clutched the mouth of the bag even tighter and lifted up his feet, propping them on the dashboard. Now I was thinking about what portion of his anatomy was currently closest to the snake, and I wasn't sure I liked it. We had heard Ohio had no poisonous serpents, so we were fairly sure this was *probably* just a harmless black rat snake. Rich said, kind of laughing, "He's really starting to move. I don't know if I can hold him."

"Quit fooling around," I told him. "This is no time to be—"

And with that, the snake's head shot up out of the bag, and it started biting Rich on the hand.

I was screaming, Rich was screaming, blood was spurting from his hand, and the snake bit down so hard it snapped off its front fangs in the flesh of Rich's thumb.

Later, comparing notes, Rich and I realized we both had the same thought: if he threw the snake out the window, it could whip back into the rear of the car, the way discarded cigarettes used to do in the old days when people smoked all the time. And the only thing worse than the situation we had right then would be to have a maddened snake running around loose in the car, even one that was now fangless and (most likely) not poisonous.

Rich grabbed that snake under its jaw and held on so tightly that the poor creature couldn't even shut its mouth, let alone move its head. It got kind of bug-eyed and seemed to be trying to tell us that it hadn't done anything wrong, it was all a misunderstanding.

By now I was flying up the highway at warp speed, and I had to brake hard to slew into a wide turn at the park entrance. We tore up the park's driveway, gravel flying, dust billowing up in great clouds behind us.

I stopped the car. There was a long moment of silence. The snake watched me closely to see what my next move might be. So did Rich. He had his seat belt tight across his chest, with one hand on the snake's body, the other holding its jaw in a death grip, and could not immediately see a safe way to get out of the car. I came around and unbuckled the seat belt, and Rich, clutching the snake's jaw even more tightly, let go of its body and leaped out of the car. With a single swift motion, he stood tall and flung the snake in the air. If serpent tossing ever becomes an Olympic event, he'll definitely make the US team. The snake flew in a long, lovely arc, landed next to the Little League field, and slithered out of our lives.

On the way back to the house, as he picked the fangs out of his hand, Rich said, "Listen, I'm ninety percent sure that was just a harmless black rat snake, but if I collapse on the plane or anything, be sure to tell them it bit me."

"Thanks for mentioning it, otherwise the whole incident could so easily have slipped my mind."

I was greatly relieved that Rich survived the flight to California, and the next day we turned in the report that was short one appendix. While I was in the middle of explaining to the client about the computer crash and the snake, the building began to tremble, and I realized we were having an earthquake.

"Okay, God," I said silently. "The computer crash, the snake, and now an earthquake. You have my attention. *What are you trying to tell me?*"

I'm still trying to work that one out.

Snakes, bats, mice, moles, deer, and other pests notwithstanding, we loved our Ohio home. We had lived there our entire married lives, it held a thousand irreplaceable memories, and — as we explained at great length to our friends and neighbors — we certainly had no intention of giving up our beloved home in order to spend a year in Seville.

I was surprised — stunned, even — at how people reacted to the news that we were going to live abroad for twelve months.

When I walked two doors down the street to tell my friend Nancy, she exploded. "Oh my God, no, I can't believe it. That's terrible news. You're leaving? I can't believe you would do this!"

I was shocked by the vehemence of her response. "But Nancy—"

She took a deep breath and threw up her hands. "Okay. I can see this thing is going to happen whether I want it to or not. I just had to get that out. How can I help?" And from then on, she could not have been more supportive.

It was a good thing I talked with Nancy early on, because her reaction helped me understand, at least a little, why some of my closest longtime friends essentially stopped speaking to me the moment they heard I was leaving. It seemed they could not get past their anger and were making a preemptive strike, abandoning me before I could abandon them. Unlike San Franciscans, who accept the transient nature of the community as the price for living in one of the world's most desirable locations, Clevelanders expect the people they love to stay in their lives for the duration. And they can get pretty bitter if they don't.

Figuring this out made their reaction less bewildering, but it didn't make my heart hurt any less. At a time when I most wanted to feel supported, when I really needed to draw my community around me like a warm and comforting shawl one more time, some of the people I loved most were looking at me as if I had just announced I was moving to Afghanistan to join al-Qaeda.

I kept trying to reconnect, taking these friends out for coffee (if they would even agree to meet) and talking about how I'd be back in a year, and in the meantime we would stay in touch by email. One woman coolly declared, "When it comes to friends, I tend to be 'out of sight, out of mind.' I don't keep up with people I don't see on a regular basis." Others promised to keep in touch, but didn't. As I was to learn over the next months, they'd respond belatedly to my chatty emails with stilted little replies they obviously took no pleasure in writing, like a thank-you note to a relative you can't stand for a gift you didn't like. With deep regret, I let these old friends slip out of my life.

Other people, including many of our relatives, were frankly bewildered. Visiting abroad was one thing, but living there? Among all those foreigners? Why would we want to? What was wrong with the good old US of A? What was wrong with us?

And then there were the friends and relatives who entered into the true spirit of the enterprise, saying, "What an adventure! You'll have to write and tell me all about it!" or, "Great, I've always wanted to visit Spain. What's the best time of year to go?" In some cases, our move enabled us to rekindle old friendships with people who lived in other parts of the country but shared our penchant for travel. People we'd kept up with only sporadically would become frequent visitors and closer friends than they'd ever been in the past.

The bottom line is, people's reactions will really, really surprise you. You never know who will stick by you, who will fall away, and who may come into your life in a whole new way.

I was still lightheaded and heavyhearted from this emotional roller coaster when we got back to Seville to start house hunting. Rich, whose friends tended to fall more into the bewildered-to-attaboy range, was less emotionally bruised and more than ready for some real estate action. We had just six weeks to find an apartment, negotiate the contract, and if possible, buy enough furnishings to make the place livable before we returned to Ohio in December.

In those days Seville was enjoying relatively prosperous times, spending European Union development money as fast as possible before it disappeared (as it would all too soon when the global economic recession hit). Crumbling old ruins were being dusted off, shored up, patched, rewired, replumbed, painted, and given new life as shops and apartments. Prices fluctuated wildly, because no one really knew what the market would bear, especially since the recent changeover from the peseta to the euro. Families hurriedly transformed their grandfather's albatross into what they hoped would be a golden goose, and speculators arrived on the scene with suitcases full of Mafia money in need of laundering. Spanish friends told us about the lowball prices they were paying, while foreigners we knew were paying two and three times that much, albeit for somewhat larger places with terraces and garages. We hoped to get something toward the lower end of the scale, not only out of natural thriftiness but because we didn't want to look like clueless rubes to our Spanish friends.

And they would know, because they would ask. It's perfectly normal for Sevillanos to say, "What a nice apartment. How much do you pay for it?" In fact, I am often gobsmacked by the highly personal and/or utterly impossible questions our Spanish friends put to us, such as "How old are you?" and "Have you gained weight?" and "Who do you think is prettier, me or my daughter?" They expect an answer; evasions are considered bad manners. Once my hairdresser asked, "You don't have any children. Is it because you don't want them or can't have them?" This was a bit forward, even for a Spanish woman, but it did lead to a discussion more interesting that the comparative merits of mousse versus hair spray.

Our real estate agent, bless her, confined herself to questions about the physical features we were looking for in an apartment and didn't delve too deeply into the personal lives we hoped to lead there. She took us to cramped and dingy rooftop apartments with vast terraces; suites in old palaces ripe with history and mold; furnished apartments that came with gruesome old couches and, in one case, a live-in landlady; and starkly modern places with hideous, liver-colored floors. While many had good features, there was always a deal breaker. The one thing the agent assured us we didn't have to worry about was bringing the dog — all apartments allow pets, she explained; you don't even have to ask about it. That was great news, but we still had to find the right place to call home.

We had just turned down a flat near the river that had little to recommend it besides a huge terrace accessible through the back of a closet, rather like the entrance to Narnia, when the real estate agent made one last suggestion. It was an old *palacio* that had recently been renovated. Granted, it didn't have all the features we wanted, such as a terrace and a nearby park, and it was smack-bang in the middle of the Alfalfa barrio, although on a quiet back street with no bars. Would we like to see it? Before

I could get "No" past my lips, Rich had already said, "Sure, why not?"

As with the Ohio house, we were goners as soon as we walked in. The apartment was large and roomy, with twelve-foot ceilings and shuttered French windows overlooking the roof of a two-hundred-year-old church. The main hallway alone was larger than some of the apartments we'd seen, and it led to a spacious living room, three modest bedrooms, two bathrooms, and a long, sunny kitchen. And the price, a little above what our Spanish friends had quoted us but well below the rent most foreigners were paying, seemed more than reasonable considering all the space. I wanted it desperately.

"What about the terrace?" I asked Rich, struggling to keep my head. "What about the park? What about the *botellones*?"

He waved it all aside. "I'll put in some window boxes. We'll walk the dog in the neighborhood. The *botellones* are streets away."

Yep, he was a goner all right.

We told the agent we'd take it.

But it wasn't that easy. Now we learned that another family had seen it first and wanted a few days to consider whether they wanted it. We would have to wait until they made up their minds. They promised to have an answer by Wednesday.

As we waited, Rich and I began building up the apartment in our minds until we felt we couldn't live without it. We forced ourselves to keep checking out other places, but they all seemed cramped and musty and second-rate. Trying to find flaws in the Alfalfa apartment, we asked each other whether the church bells right outside our windows might be deafening. Standing next to the church at various times, we soon discovered they only rang the bells once a day, before morning mass, and they were among the quietest bells in the city. Still concerned about the *botellones*, I asked our friend Luz what she thought of the neighborhood.

"The Alfalfa area is great," she said. "And the best thing about it is that you never have to worry about coming home late at night, because with all the *botellones*, there will always be people around." And here I had been thinking that hundreds of drunken youths might be a security problem!

As usual, Luz turned out to be right. Spanish young people are far too busy drinking, flirting, and trying to impress each other to pay attention to oldsters like us. And unlike their American counterparts, these young people don't seem inclined to become gangs of hooligans on the rampage. Fistfights might occasionally break out, but violence isn't a major feature of the night's entertainment. I read about one huge *botellón* that drew a crowd of five thousand kids; they spent all night drinking, and there wasn't a single arrest. I was almost sorry when Seville eventually passed a law banning *botellones* in the Alfalfa neighborhood; of course, it's largely ignored, so there is still plenty of company around the barrio late at night.

When I finally heard back from the agent, it was to learn that the other family needed a few more days to make up their minds; she hoped to let us know on Friday. I thanked her politely, hung up, and spent the next few hours seething with frustration. Finally I pulled myself together and came up with an idea.

"We need help," I told Rich. "We need an expert. We need San Pancracio."

If you've never heard of San Pancracio (St. Pancras), you're not alone. Except for St. Pancras Station in London, he's virtually disappeared from the world's memory except in Seville, where his image can be found in nearly every bar, restaurant, café, food shop, and market stall in the city, as well as many homes, offices, and taxis. The statues show him as a long-haired teenager in a red and green toga, one arm holding a book, the other upraised as if hailing a cab. If you look closely, you'll usually find a sprig of fresh parsley at his feet.

San Pancracio was a fourteen-year-old martyr killed in the fourth century for preaching Christianity (unsuccessfully) to a Roman emperor. By rights he should be the patron saint of adolescents being impertinent to their elders, but then, the church's logic in these matters is often inscrutable. For reasons best known to themselves, church elders designated him the patron saint of health and work, and while nobody can tell you where the parsley tradition comes from, thousands of fresh sprigs are placed daily at his feet.

San Pancracio would probably have remained just another Seville curiosity for me if it hadn't been for some bad news we'd received the year before about a friend who had just been diagnosed with pancreatic cancer. This is almost invariably a swift and fatal disease, and we were casting about for something that might cheer him up when it occurred to us we could bring him back an image of San Pancracio. Who could be better to help with the health of the pancreas? Our friend surprised everyone by living on for years, a "miracle" that we jokingly attributed to the saint's intervention.

Worried about losing the apartment, I decided this would be a good time to ask San Pancracio for another "miracle." I collected our small plastic statue of him, some parsley from the kitchen, a candle left over from a romantic dinner. To assemble an altar was for me but the work of a moment. I even put a few coins down and promised more if the saint came through.

"That ought to do it," I told Rich. "You can stop worrying. When the agent calls day after tomorrow, I'm sure it will be good news."

I was wrong in one respect: the agent called the very next morning at nine thirty (an impossibly early hour by Sevillano standards) to let us know the apartment was ours. We were wild with joy, doing a victory dance around the room, thanking the saint for coming through once again.

Do I really think San Pancracio made the difference? Of course not. I'm a modern woman and consider that sort of voodoo Catholicism to be a relic of the Dark Ages. All the same, I still slip San Pan a few euros whenever I have a special cause, and I consider the twenty bucks I put into his shrine's money box just before a key election to be some of the best money I've ever spent.

Whether or not the saint helped seal the deal, we shook hands on it with our new landlord, and while he went away to draw up the papers, Rich and I started thinking seriously about furnishings. Our lovely new home was not only totally lacking in furniture, it was missing several key *electrodomésticos* (major appliances) such as refrigerator, oven, and washing machine. Transport from the US was far too costly for us to consider bringing anything beyond the few keepsakes we could carry on the plane. We would have to do a *lot* of shopping.

I loved the idea of furnishing a new home from scratch. Like most couples, we'd accumulated our furniture piecemeal, combining the possessions we brought into the relationship (with a little tactful weeding out on both sides) and adding new pieces as things wore out or our living patterns changed. Here, we'd need everything from wine glasses to sofas. But with a stay of only a year, it would be ridiculous to invest heavily in new household goods and furnishings. We set out like impoverished newlyweds to see what we could purchase on a shoestring.

My first thought was secondhand furniture shops, but I quickly discovered that in Seville, castoffs go to friends and acquaintances or are put out in the street near the trash bins for the neighbors, homeless, and gypsies to pick over. Luckily, Seville had a new Ikea outside of town, a handful of unfinished-furniture sellers, and a street of hip little décor shops with reasonable prices. We haunted them all, with side trips to stores selling discount *electrodomésticos* and the kinds of tools Rich felt were indispensable to home maintenance. In the space of three weeks, we ordered an entire apartment's worth of furniture and appliances, all to be delivered the following week as soon as the contract was signed. We would then have a week to get the apartment in order before returning to the US.

The Spanish like to leave things until the last minute, so we weren't seriously alarmed that we had ordered thousands of dollars' worth of furnishings without ever having seen the lease. We kept asking about it, and finally we got our hands on a copy the day before we were supposed to sign it and take possession of the keys. The document's dense Spanish legalese wasn't easy to decipher, but one phrase jumped out at us with hideous clarity: "No pets allowed."

In a near panic, I called our real estate agent, who arranged an emergency meeting with the landlord. He explained that the previous renter had owned a dog that annoyed the other tenants with its barking, messes in the hallway, and generally pestilential behavior. Tired of hearing the complaints, the landlord swore that from now on pets would be prohibited in the building, starting with our lease. None of the previous leases had placed any restrictions on pets. And here our landlord got crafty. He said he would allow us to have our dog here if, and only if, we could get all three of the other tenants to sign a document giving up their right to have a pet in their apartment.

Why in God's name would they ever sign such a document? What would motivate total strangers to give up an existing right to benefit us? This would never work. But it was a take-it-or-leave-it deal, so we reluctantly agreed.

Naturally, I made another donation to San Pancracio to interest him in the case. That done, we hung around the building ringing the other buzzers in an attempt to catch our new neighbors at home. The first one we caught up with said, "Sure I'll sign. This document means nothing. If I want an elephant in my apartment I'll have one. It's my right." The other two shared his opinion, and all three signed without hesitation and, in the Spanish manner, with lots of flourishes. We brought their signatures back to the landlord, and soon our own, more modest signatures were on the lease agreement.

So Rich, the dog, and I had a home. The delivery trucks arrived, and after the sweating *repartidores* had dragged all the boxes into the elevator and hauled the bed and couches up the stairs, we had furniture and appliances too. Now all we had to do was return to Ohio for Christmas, collect the visas and the dog, and fly back to Seville in January to begin our year of living abroad.

Chapter 4

LOST IN TRANSIT: ONE DOG

❧

While Rich and I had long discussions debating the rival merits of just about every aspect of the move, one thing was a given from the start: our dog, Pie, would be coming with us. For nearly ten years, Pie had been making it abundantly clear that she did not approve of us gallivanting around the globe without her. Normally the most cheerful of creatures, she became deeply disturbed whenever she saw the suitcases come out of the attic. She would give us The Look, an expression of such wounded betrayal it was all I could do not to cancel the plane reservations. As I started packing my clothes, she would run and get her favorite toy and place it gently in the suitcase with my things. Then she would turn to look up at me with such a pitiful, hopeful expression it just made me want to slit my wrists.

It was a terrific performance. And even though I absolutely knew that within five minutes of our departure she would be partying hearty with the house sitter and never give us a passing thought until we returned, it was hard to resist. Pie was the best hustler I ever met.

She started out life in a litter of puppies that was abandoned in a cardboard box by the side of the freeway in downtown Cleveland. While the litter was en route to the county pound, which was overflowing with dogs whose days were numbered, a woman from a dog rescue organization impulsively decided to take one of the abandoned puppies home, and naturally Pie made sure she was the one selected. The woman then decided she didn't really need another dog, since she already had twenty-seven of them living in her modest suburban home; I have always pictured the house and its small yard as a canine version of the movie *Soylent Green*. Deciding not to keep number twenty-eight, the woman left the puppy with a guy she knew at a dog show, where we happened to see her and knew instantly she was the one for us. All puppies are cute at seven weeks, but Pie had that extra dollop of adorability that made even the most hardened observer's voice go up an octave. She was irresistible, she knew it, and she worked it for all it was worth.

Her breed? The prevailing theory was part border collie, part springer spaniel. She was about knee high, with long hair in black, red-brown, and white, rather like a cross between a border collie and a Saint Bernard. Her Nordic look and sweet personality suggested the name Eskimo Pie; for short she was Pie, Pi, or 3.1416.

Pie was a total extrovert. She never met a stranger, just new best friends. Every day was a party; every night was New Year's Eve. Most mornings I simply let her out the back door after breakfast and let her make her own arrangements for the day, which would usually include chasing animals in the woods, napping under her favorite bush, and wheedling food out of any workmen doing projects in the neighborhood. She was such a chow hound, I knew she'd always turn up in time for supper.

Pie was a great forager, and her eclectic appetite included vegetables swiped from the garden (she particularly liked snow peas) as well as more conventional fare, such as pet food pilfered from neighbors' back porches and the occasional slow-moving squirrel. One particularly frenetic day during the Christmas holidays, a gift package arrived in the mail just as Rich and I were heading out to the movies, and not having time to open it, I tossed the box under the tree on my way out the door. Hours later we arrived home to find Pie lying on her back under the Christmas tree, paws in the air, a blissful expression on her face. It turned out the package had contained a rum cake, and she had ripped open the box and devoured the entire thing. She was fat, drunk, and happy for three days. I'm sure it was one of her most cherished holiday memories.

Pie used her charm and joie de vivre to enslave our various house sitters, and she benefitted handsomely from their lavish attentions, enjoying long walks in the snowy woods, play dates with other dogs, and special food, often distributed directly from the table in a serious breach of house rules. Pie once spent three happy months with a house sitter named Mike while Rich and I were doing a volunteer work assignment in the former Soviet republic of Georgia. Shortly before we were scheduled to return, Mike took Pie in for professional grooming.

"Shall I give her a trim, bring out her lines a little?" the groomer asked.

"Sure," said Mike, thinking she meant to tidy up a few wisps here and there. Two hours later, he returned to find that our lovely, fluffy dog had been shaved from head to tail. "I actually screamed," he told us later.

"Don't you like it?" asked the groomer.

"But she's a long-haired dog," cried Mike. "Her tail is like a weeping willow. Where's the willow? *Where's the willow?*"

In a condition bordering on hysteria, he sent us an email. "Pie decided she needed a new look for spring," he wrote. "And don't worry, it'll grow. The only thing is, it makes her look more like a male dog than a female."

Arriving home prepared for the worst, we decided she looked adorable, if a little butch, with three-quarters of an inch of hair. But our real worry was now that she'd gotten away with shaving her head and body, what would be next — a nose ring and a tattoo?

Actually, it was a microchip.

When I began the arduous task of organizing the logistics of Pie's transport and immigration to Spain, I was relieved to learn that she would not have to go into quarantine so long as I filled out a stack of paperwork, made sure all her shots were current, and had a microchip implanted in her shoulder. The microchip sounded intriguing at first, but I soon discovered it would not actually make her a remote-control dog or give her bionic powers; it was just an ID chip the size of a grain of rice that would be injected into her shoulder and could be read with a special wand.

I consulted the vet, government officials, and the chip manufacturer to make sure the one I was getting was compatible with international standards and would enable Pie to pass through customs in Spain. They all reassured me this was indeed the chip I needed. Once it was inserted, I was given the chip's serial number; but when I tried to enter it in the necessary forms, I discovered it had the wrong number of digits. When I called the manufacturer, I was told, "Oh, that chip won't work *overseas*. You need a different kind of chip for that. Unfortunately, we can't sell you one of those, because they're illegal in the US."

Apparently the powerful pet microchip lobby had convinced the United States government that it's vital to American interests that we use a different kind of chip from the rest of the planet. Thank heavens these public-spirited citizens are vigorously protecting our borders against any attempts to introduce foreign chips into the lucrative pet-chip market in this great nation of ours.

Was I annoyed about this? Don't get me started. Words were exchanged, but in the end there was nothing to do but drive Pie to Canada (which luckily was only a day trip from Cleveland) so she could get an international chip inserted into her other shoulder.

My next task was calling around to various airlines to arrange her transport. A representative of Iberia, the Spanish airline, said, "You're bringing your *dog*? Can't you leave it at home?"

I explained we were moving to Spain and wanted her with us.

"If I were you, I'd make other arrangements," she said darkly. "It's not good for dogs to travel by air. They're cold, they're frightened, they're upset, they get sick, they get loose, they get out on the runway, they get killed..."

If that's what I was hearing from the *customer relations department* — the people paid to put the best possible face on the company's track record — clearly I'd better scratch Iberia off the short list. And it was a very short list; most airlines don't let pets travel in the coldest months, and we were planning to leave in January.

I finally found a major US airline that claimed to have a heated cargo area for pets and booked all three of us on flights from Cleveland to Newark to Madrid. Pie was not allowed to bring any toys, have any food or water, or take any medicines to make her sleep. However, for a mere $110 extra, the airline offered to walk Pie for ten minutes in Newark. It seemed pricy for a pee, but we agreed to pay it. It was going to be a long trip; with the advance loading time of three hours, a two-hour flight to Newark, a two-hour layover there, and eight hours to Madrid, Pie was looking at a minimum of fifteen hours in her crate.

I spent much of November and December assembling Pie's paperwork, which included documenting her health history, certifying she'd received every vaccine known to veterinary medicine, and providing proof of both microchips and their serial numbers. We were also busy assembling our own travel papers, and Rich kept calling the Spanish consulate in Chicago to ask when our residency visas would be ready. They kept promising them soon, soon... As December rolled on toward January, our calls to Chicago become more frequent and more urgent. Finally one of our calls brought the welcome news that the process was complete; all we had to do was fly to Chicago in person with our passports to pick up our visas.

In Chicago, the consular staff inserted small, official-looking pieces of paper into our passports. Just as Rich and I were breathing a sigh of relief, the agent added, "And when you get to Seville, you must of course take this to the Foreigners' Office to apply for your residency visa."

What? We thought we'd just done that. What *had* they been doing with our paperwork for the last six months, reading it aloud to each other to practice their English?

The consular staff responded to our confusion and alarm by assuring us this was the natural order of events. Our *preliminary* paperwork had been processed in Chicago. Our passports now contained this little slip of paper that, while apparently not an actual visa, was akin to one, and all we had to do was resubmit all our paperwork once we got to the Foreigners' Office in Seville.

We took what comfort we could from these slender assurances and returned to Ohio to begin packing. At least, we told ourselves, we could forget about the paperwork issues until we got back to Spain.

Wrong again. The day before our departure, the consulate called to inform us that they had forgotten to give us a crucial piece of the not-quite-a-visa paperwork. What to do? There was no time for us to return to fetch it, and after much discussion (which may have gotten just a trifle heated on our part), they reluctantly agreed to FedEx it to us — at our expense, of course. It would arrive by ten thirty the next morning, and we didn't have to leave for the airport until noon. Not a problem.

We awoke the next morning to near-blizzard conditions. Between the blowing snow and the glowering skies, visibility was dismal and the road conditions were slushy and treacherous despite the best efforts of the township's snowplow crews. We paced around in the living room, circling the pile of our luggage and Pie's enormous crate, peering out the windows in hopes of seeing the familiar orange and purple logo of the FedEx truck emerging through the thickening snow. Calls to the airport confirmed our departing flight was on schedule, even if the famously reliable FedEx was not.

Our intrepid friend Dorothy, who was providing airport transport, called to say she was on her way over to collect us. At quarter to twelve, we saw headlights turn into the drive. Two sets of headlights: the FedEx truck rolled up to the front door with Dorothy's SUV following closely behind. We grabbed the package from the FedEx driver, shoved it into our carry-on luggage, and stowed everything, including Pie and her crate, in Dorothy's SUV. We were off.

At the airline's cargo area, we unloaded the crate (in which we had secreted one of her favorite small toys, to hell with regulations) and coaxed Pie into it. As I walked away, I didn't need to glance back to know that The Look was boring into my back.

From our seats on the plane, Rich and I watched through the window as Pie's crate trundled up the luggage belt into the plane's hold. We saw her unloaded in Newark, hoped that someone would actually extract her from the crate for her high-priced ten-minute walk, and later observed the crate being reloaded onto the plane that would take us all to Spain. Eight hours later, Rich and I stumbled down the jet bridge in Madrid and asked the first airline representative we saw where to go to collect the dog.

No one knew. In fact, no one could even begin to guess whom we could go ask for a conjecture about where we might begin to look for her. "¿*Una perra?*" they all said blankly. "A dog? Here? Really?" I was beginning to see what the woman from Iberia Air was talking about. Was Pie wandering around the runways even as we spoke? Had she died en route and been secreted away by the customer relations department? Was she already on her way to the North Pole or back to Cleveland?

In a real crisis, a sort of calm descends over me. Facing situations where any woman of normal sensibility would be crying or shouting or phoning her lawyer, I channel all my emotions into a sort of fierce hyperefficiency mode. "Don't worry," I said to Rich through gritted teeth. "We will find her."

The Madrid airport is huge, with multiple terminals and signage clearly designed to conceal rather than impart information. Rich and I combed every one of the terminals, asking everyone we could find for suggestions as to where we could go look for our dog. No one could even hazard a guess, but we did learn there were cargo areas that spread for kilometers in every direction around the airport, so after two hours of fruitless inquiries, we rented a car and started driving. We went from cargo terminal to cargo terminal, showing Pie's transit papers to bored clerks who just shrugged and told us to try someplace else.

I kept thinking about a story my mother often told of her childhood, about the day one of her beloved dogs ran off during a roadside stop en route to a horse show at Coronado. Her mother, she always said, had been wonderful, throwing herself into the search, hunting everywhere. But as time passed, my grandmother grew increasingly frantic about getting to the horse show, and eventually she decided they had to leave the missing dog and go on. Fifty years later my mother was still haunted by the memory. I was haunted by it now.

Wearily I walked into yet another cargo building, this one a good four kilometers from the airport, and waved my papers under the nose of yet another uninterested clerk. "*Busco una perra*," I said. (I am looking for a dog...)

The clerk glanced over the papers. "You'll need to fill out this form, and this, and this," he said, pushing yet more papers over to me.

"What? She's here?"

"And you'll need the vet to sign and stamp the papers."

"But she's here?"

"First, you need to fill out the papers..."

In a haze of joyful relief, I began scribbling and waited while the clerk arranged for a vet to come certify that Pie was fit to enter the country. Twenty minutes later, I heard the rumble of a forklift approaching. As it drew near I saw, cradled in its metal arms, Pie's crate.

Pie was on her feet with her nose pressed against the bars of her crate and a fierce gleam in her eye.

"I have no idea where you've brought me," she seemed to be saying, "but wherever it is, it damn well better be good."

Chapter 5

SETTLING IN

❦

"She ate an entire *kilo* of *sugar?*" Rich exclaimed.

"No, only about half of it," I said, trying to sound reassuring. "Looks like she managed to tear open one of those little bags of olives too."

It's not easy for a dog to look green, but Pie was managing it. Rich and I, toting bags of groceries, had arrived back at our Seville apartment to find her in the kitchen, standing rather unsteadily beside the open cupboard door, surrounded by scattered sugar and olives and shreds of paper and plastic. I thought I'd put all the food up high enough to escape her reach, but apparently not. Days after the overseas flight, Pie was probably still suffering from some canine version of jet lag, but her appetite and foraging skills seemed to have survived the trip in good working order.

"Come on, Pie," I said, snapping the leash onto her collar. "I'd better get you outside." We made it down the two long flights of stairs and out into the street before she disgraced herself, which was something to be thankful for.

Pie was not finding it entirely easy to adapt to her new life. She wasn't used to being inside so much of the day, on marble floors that made her slip and sometimes, if she moved too fast, slide ignominiously into a door or wall. Whenever she did go outside, instead of running free in the woods, she had to be on a leash so I could haul her back from the path of oncoming cars. In the Ohio countryside she'd treated cars we encountered on the road with great respect, but when they were flashing by all around her, she couldn't figure out what was safe. And with no woods or even lawn about, she couldn't tell where she was supposed to take care of her most basic functions. After she realized the other dogs just used the sidewalk, she got *too* relaxed about it and started going in places I really wished she wouldn't, such as the steps of churches or among the tables of the better sidewalk cafés. Eventually, after I'd shouted, "No, Pie, no!" a thousand times, we worked out habits we both could live with.

Fortunately, there were many features of life in Seville that she took to with ease and delight, among them riding in the elevator. When the doors opened on arrival, she'd always flash me a big, doggy grin as if to say, "Did ya see that? It did it *again!*"

She loved late-night walks through the city and was elated to be allowed into bars and cafés, where she could browse through the greasy napkins on the floor for bits of dropped ham and chorizo before curling up at our feet for a nap. I used to pour water from my glass into a saucer and place it on the floor for her to drink, until I realized that the barmen and waitresses were scandalized by this behavior. Even though we all knew the dishes would be put through the fierce chemicals and hot water of an industrial-strength dishwashing machine — I could often watch the dishes being loaded into it from where I sat — the Spanish universally consider any contact between a plate and a dog's mouth to be horribly unhygienic, tantamount to letting the beast slobber on platters of food being carried from kitchen to customers. Even using an ashtray for her water made them visibly upset. I soon learned to ask for a disposable plastic container, which they were happy enough to provide.

Trying to fathom local attitudes toward hygiene is always tricky. Shortly before we flew back to Ohio to collect Pie, Rich and I stumbled across a tiny Mexican café near Seville's main river and decided to give it a try. We were sampling some sauce-covered cheese that was attempting to pass itself off as a quesadilla when I glanced at the next table and saw one of the women leaning over a stroller, changing her baby's diapers. Just then, the waiter arrived at their table with plates of food, and as soon as his hands were free, the woman calmly passed him the dirty diaper for disposal. Without the slightest appearance of discomfort, the waiter whisked it away.

My jaw dropped.

"Kind of gives a whole new meaning to the phrase 'family-style restaurant,' doesn't it?" Rich said.

While this was unusual even for Spain, the norms here *are* different. It's quite common for parents of toddlers to pull down their pants (come *on*, you know I mean the *kids'* pants) in public places so the little ones can pee on the grass or dirt around a tree. At Christmas, the larger Nativity scenes nearly always include, somewhere in the background, a tiny crouched figure who is clearly, explicitly defecating; they say it's to add a touch of earthy realism. Just last December some enterprising artisans introduced a new Nativity figure that urinated a tiny stream of real water; the supply sold out overnight.

The Sevillanos have a keen sense of humor and a down-to-earth attitude about the essentials of daily life. And now that I was living among them on a full-time basis, I was working hard, just like Pie, to come up to speed on the often surprising customs of my new world. It had been one thing to come and go, creating a hybrid lifestyle that mixed American and Spanish ways, but now I threw myself into learning how to fit in with my new community as much as possible. I wanted to feel at home here. I wanted to belong.

But as Maslow was fond of pointing out, the hierarchy of human needs means you start on the ground floor with food and shelter before turning your attention to higher goals, such as belonging. So my very earliest priority was checking out the nearby food markets. I discovered a dozen within easy walking distance, including tiny produce shops, hole-in-the-wall delicatessens, and several chains that call themselves supermarkets but are barely a tenth the size of their American counterparts. These "supermarkets" stock a lot of useful packaged goods, such as milk that doesn't need to be refrigerated until it's opened, but often their fruits and vegetables look as if they were repeatedly struck with a hammer and left in the trunk of a car for a few weeks before being displayed for sale. There was also a large farmers' market, where shoppers still buy whole rabbits in their fur, mesh bags of wriggling snails, and an array of terrifying and mysterious sea creatures, along with a wide range of wholesome and recognizable produce, fish, meat, and cheese. For exotic foreign luxuries such as peanut butter and maple syrup, there was the huge supermarket in the basement of the big department store, El Corte Inglés. I had plenty of choices; the only real limitation was how much I could carry home without a car, and soon I fell into the habit of shopping for groceries on a daily basis.

Shopping daily was a great help, since our food storage capacity was limited to a single narrow cabinet and the modest refrigerator we bought. The apartment came with a four-burner stovetop but no oven, which is typical in Seville; the women here almost never bake, preferring to leave the task to professionals who can whip up the frothy, bland desserts that are local favorites. Having grown up making cakes, cookies, and pies at my mother's knee, I couldn't imagine a kitchen that never smelled of baking, and Rich was not about to let a single holiday season pass without roasting turkey with all the trimmings. After some scouting around, we found an oven small enough to fit under our stovetop. From then on we ordered turkeys based on the dimensions of the oven rather than how many pounds or kilos we wanted.

While regular ovens are rare, microwaves are commonplace. When we bought one, I was taken aback to discover that it came with a hand-cranked dial rather than a digitally accurate timer. In the US, microwave timers are calibrated to the nanosecond; you could operate a NASA countdown with one. On the other end of the spectrum, my typical Spanish model has a dial marked in minutes that stops randomly anywhere during the last sixty seconds. Having a plus or minus factor of fifty-nine seconds when your most frequent functions are heating milk for tea (thirty seconds) and reheating cold tea (sixty seconds) renders the timer all but useless. Still, the microwave oven gets the job done, so I can't complain. I just have to watch it a little more carefully to make sure the milk doesn't boil over.

So we outfitted the kitchen with what we considered the essentials and decided against adding a garbage disposal or dishwasher. Rich, who does most of the washing up, said he liked the simplicity of doing things the old-fashioned way. In a similar frame of mind, while we did purchase an inexpensive washing machine, we followed the local custom of hanging clothes on the *azotea* (rooftop terrace) to dry. Feeling like a throwback to my grandmother's generation, I began watching the weather reports to decide when it was safe to do a wash, then hauling baskets of wet clothes and bed linens up onto the roof. On typically warm days, the Seville sun dries laundry in half the time it takes my dryer back in the US; on the downside, it can bake the color right out of black cotton underwear, leaving it as gray and nearly as rough as old asphalt. In rainy winter weather, we have to drape the wet laundry on a portable rack next to a space heater and wait days for the jeans to dry.

Our wash water is heated as needed in a small, wall-mounted tank fueled by a *bombona de butano* (butane tank) that has to be replaced every few weeks. The *bombona* delivery men, known as *butaneros*, are famously elusive, arriving early Monday mornings, stashing their truck down an alley or on a sidewalk, then disappearing into apartment buildings to drop off tanks to favored customers of long standing. In the early days, the first half of my Monday morning walk with Pie was often spent running around looking for the *butaneros* and convincing them to haul a *bombona* up to our apartment. Like so much else in Seville, it was a matter of *enchufe*, literally being "plugged in" to the system. Rather than spending months convincing the *butaneros* that we were not fly-by-night foreigners but long-term customers worth cultivating, we resorted to simple bribery. When the *butaneros* realized we were deliberately overpaying by a euro each time and were good for a handsome tip at Christmas, they began ringing our doorbell every Monday and showing up on the doorstep with alacrity and a *bombona*.

As we were finding ways to take care of our most basic needs, such as food, sleep, and cleanliness, we were also adapting to the Sevillano schedule for these and other activities of daily living. The Spanish, especially those in southern Spain, are famous for eating late at night, usually around ten. But that's just the tip of the iceberg. The entire daily round is different, and if you are out of sync with it, you'll miss out on most of the fun. I've had guests who refuse to take a siesta, denouncing it as wasting the best part of the day. Left to their own devices, they rise at dawn to photograph tourist sites, eat lunch at noon among a scattering of locals having a late second breakfast, wander alone through the empty streets during the hottest part of the day, dine early in a deserted restaurant and go to bed just when locals are gathering for the first beer of the evening. And then they wonder aloud why Seville has such a jolly reputation when they found it rather dull.

When we made the commitment to live in Seville, Rich and I began keeping Sevillano hours. The adjustment went surprisingly smoothly. Whereas in Ohio I would spring up at six, here I ease out of bed about eight in the morning. Many locals start with a light breakfast, sometimes just a cup of *café con leche* (coffee with milk); my "first breakfast" is a big mug of hot, milky tea. As I sip it, I check emails, write, or do other work, then I sit down with Rich for some cereal around ten, a time when many Sevillanos are having their second breakfast of coffee and toast, often out in a café. After this more substantial breakfast, I continue with my day: writing, painting, going to the gym, shopping, meeting friends, doing errands. About two o'clock I make lunch, which is our main meal of the day, and then Rich and I take our siestas.

As everyone knows, siestas evolved as a practical strategy for surviving intense summer heat, which in Seville means 120-degree temperatures for weeks at a time, making it dangerous as well as uncomfortable to be outside from midday until well past dark. I've tried walking in Seville during an August afternoon, and it left me gasping, flushed, soaked with sweat, and wondering how long it takes for blood to actually boil in your veins. The

Sevillanos are right: my best option — *everyone's* best option — is to sleep in the early afternoon, at least on blazing hot days, which can pop up sporadically as early as March, are pretty much a given from June through mid-September, and can trickle in through October.

Over the centuries, the habit of siesta became thoroughly ingrained in the culture, a fixed part of the daily routine even in winter. Although Seville winters are comparatively mild, temperatures can drop to around freezing, and most older buildings, like ours, have woefully inadequate heating. A month or two after we'd brought Pie to Seville, when the weather was still quite chilly, Luz took us to her sister's house in the country. We spent a pleasant morning tramping around the grounds looking at pigs and sheep, followed by a hearty lunch in front of the kitchen fireplace. After the meal our hostess announced, "Now, we sleep." She led us into a cold, dark parlor, where eight or ten armchairs were drawn up around what looked like a round dining table covered with a heavy velvet cloth. This was an old-fashioned *mesa camilla*, a traditional table with a heater (in the olden days, a brazier of coals) underneath. We each chose an armchair, tucked our feet up on the wooden ring around the heater, and drew the thick velvet onto our laps like blankets. As I nestled into my chair, a heavenly warmth stole over me. I was just slipping into a blissful doze when our host began to snore like a trumpeting bull. I soon abandoned all hope of sleeping, and when others began rising from their chairs and tiptoeing out to the kitchen, I gave up and joined them there.

I may have missed out on my afternoon sleep that day, but when I'm in Spain I rarely go without my siesta. Even during our shorter spring visits to the city, I had taken instantly to the idea of relaxing and dozing after lunch, a luxury I'd never been able to indulge in back in the US. Working as a writer, graphic designer, consultant, and volunteer, I was forever on deadline and powered on through days that often lasted from six in the morning to ten at night. I would feel like a total slacker if, after inhaling a carton of yogurt for lunch, I relaxed for ten minutes with a book before booting up my computer again. In Seville, the city basically shuts down from two until five. You're supposed to walk home, linger over a hearty meal with your family, and then set aside your day's burdens to rest and sleep.

When we established ourselves in the apartment, I soon developed the habit of taking my postprandial ease on the living room couch. I prop myself up on the sofa cushions, staying cool on hot days with a loose cotton sundress and a fan or air conditioner; in the winter I wrap up in a thick faux-fur blanket against the chill. I read a little, and when I feel sleepy, I let myself doze off...

I usually snooze for about twenty minutes, which I've been told is typical and is the amount recommended by Spain's public health officials. Rich, who has the enviable ability to sleep anytime, anywhere, for any duration, usually gets forty minutes or so of shut-eye. After siesta, we both awaken rested, refreshed, and ready to get on with the day.

American friends often object to siestas by saying that napping during the day makes them groggy; worse, they're worried it could prevent them from sleeping properly that night. Until I moved to Spain, I had never noticed how fearful we all are in the US about not getting sufficient sleep. I've read all sorts of articles in the popular press about how we're becoming a nation of sleep-deprived zombies, whose 24/7 lifestyles and nervous insomnia are leading to poor health, lower productivity, driving accidents, less sex, more obesity, mood swings, memory impairment... and

I forget what else. In 2002 an article in the peer-reviewed medical journal *Archives of General Psychiatry* reported on a major study undertaken by the University of California, San Diego, involving more than a million people aged thirty-two to one hundred four. Researchers found that those who routinely get just six or seven hours of sleep a night actually live longer than those who manage a solid eight. Did anybody listen? No, because our entrenched cultural beliefs insist that anything less than eight hours of sack time is hazardous to your health.

The Sevillanos love their sleep as much as anybody else, but they are not afraid to sacrifice some of it in a good cause. Not for work, of course. But for their social lives? Absolutely. During the week-long, all-night drinking and dancing fest known as the Feria de Abril (April Fair), they reportedly get an average of two hours of sleep a night. And yet they show up for work the next day, find time for a siesta, and are somehow back at the fairgrounds again by dinnertime, looking radiant and ready to party on. Of course, I wouldn't advise scheduling elective surgery, car repairs, or even a manicure that week, since I doubt anyone is operating at peak efficiency; but cranky, fat, brain-dead, sexless zombies they're not.

I have rarely, if ever, heard a Sevillano complain about lack of sleep. The general attitude seems to be, "Oh well, it was worth it." They assume they will survive some short-sleep nights without any trouble, so they do. I've adopted a similar attitude, and if my energy is at a lower ebb than usual, I take comfort from the fact that thanks to the siesta, I only have to keep up the momentum of my day for seven hours at a stretch, not fourteen or sixteen.

So I took to the siesta like Pie took to chance-dropped chorizo. And it was equally easy to fall into the custom of enjoying the traditional post-siesta *merienda* (afternoon snack).

Most Spaniards I know have coffee and something sweet to reenergize them for the long evening ahead. I'm not much of a coffee drinker, especially that late in the day, but I do enjoy a *merienda* of yogurt, cookies, or fruit, sometimes with green tea. In fact, it's tantamount to a third breakfast. So I now get fourteen mornings a week, with something like twenty-one breakfasts. For a morning person like me, it's great to keep starting the day over at all hours.

Sadly, modern business practices and the standardized work schedule promoted by the European Union are gradually eroding the practice of siestas in parts of the business community. Cafés, restaurants, and some major tourist attractions stay open, as do a few food markets, the big downtown stores, and the new wave of Chinese-owned discount bazaars. And much as I am opposed to these places remaining open in defiance of siesta tradition, I confess it's mighty convenient to be able to run an errand or two when returning home late for lunch, or to keep on shopping a little longer when I'm on a roll.

Everything reopens from five until eight or nine, and by closing time, people start thinking about heading to the bars. Rich and I soon found we liked going out for a beer and a few tapas about nine in the evenings, perching on barstools and enjoying the vibrancy of the chattering crowds or sitting at a sidewalk café table with Pie at our feet, watching hopefully for a careless hand to bring a morsel of something interesting within reach. She was trained not to beg or snatch, but anything that fell to the ground was fair game, and she was alert and ready to take full advantage of her opportunities. After dinner we might stroll home around eleven; or, as we got to know more people and began meeting them in the evenings, we might stay out until anywhere from midnight to four in the morning — an hour that back in Ohio would nearly be time to rise and start the day all over again.

When we were first establishing ourselves in Seville, I had trouble staying awake for these long evenings and found myself yawning by half past eleven and visibly drooping by one o'clock. But I refused to wimp out; I wanted to fit into the city's social life, and clearly late hours were an important feature. I soon developed four simple but effective protocols: (1) drink tea or even a little coffee ahead of time; (2) eat some dessert, however bland or fattening, for the energy-boosting sugar rush; (3) drink water to dilute the alcohol and avoid dehydration, which increases feelings of tiredness; and (4) try hard not to think, "I really should be home in bed by now." I learned how to get into the zone, accepting that I was going to be at this party or bar *forever*. That way, when the group would finally break up at two or three in the morning, it would always come as a pleasant surprise. "We're going home? Already? Ah, well, if we must..."

So the Spanish hours, which at first seemed rather daunting, actually proved remarkably easy to adapt to. They make sense with the climate and are reinforced every day by long-entrenched social and business customs. The real challenge during my early days in Seville was the Spanish bureaucracy, most especially the mind-numbing tangles of byzantine procedures in the government offices handling our residency visas.

It took but a single visit to discern that the *Oficina de Extranjeros* (Foreigners' Office) that handled such matters was a masterpiece of inefficiency and muddle. Upon arrival, we waited in line to visit a windowed booth, where we would explain our business as best we could with our minimal Spanish. The clerk would then hand us a numbered pink, white, or green ticket, the color indicating our destination bureaucrat and the number identifying our place at the end of a very long line. The meaning of the different colors appeared to change inscrutably between one visit and the next, so I was never sure I had the right ticket that would lead to an audience with the person at the correct desk. The error would, of course, be revealed only when my ticket number was called after I had spent four hours sitting on a hard plastic chair in a hot, airless, overcrowded waiting room.

When we did manage to make our way to the proper authority, the conversations took on a sort of Alice-in-Wonderland quality. We'd present a document — say, Rich's pension statement. The clerk would stare at it in puzzlement and disbelief, as if we'd offered him a racy etching, then thrust it back at us, clearly wanting no part of it. Three months and several visits later, we'd be told the whole process was being held up because — fools that we were — we had failed to attach Rich's pension statement.

Eventually we convinced them to accept every possible document attesting to our financial, physical, and legal status, along with photos, fingerprints, and certification that we'd gone to the bank and paid two different fees (about twenty-four euros, or nearly thirty dollars, in all). At last, unable to think of another roadblock, the clerk finally handed over our long-term residency cards, informing us they would be good for one year from the date we first started the application process. This meant — Rich thumbed through the papers to check the starting date — they would expire in about two months.

In the meantime, Rich and I were honing our bureaucratic and linguistic skills as we struggled with lesser forms of red tape, such as establishing a bank account, which took an entire morning and left us totally confused. The bank we chose was a well-known American bank, and the staff assured us that an account with them would serve to *facilitar* transfers of funds from the US. By about three hours into the sign-up procedure, we had learned that international transfers would not be any faster, require any less paperwork, or cost any less than at other banks. I began to wonder if *facilitar* was one of those "false amigo" words our dictionary warned us about; maybe it only sounded like "facilitate" but actually meant something quite different, like "We'll treat you the same way as everyone else; what makes you think you're so special?"

The next shocking revelation was that the bank would not be paying us any interest on our savings account. In fact, many Spaniards actually have to pay the bank a fee to hold and use their money, although luckily a slightly different configuration of accounts allowed us to avoid this fate. I learned that by Spanish law, a percentage of each account in a *caja de ahorros* (savings bank) has to be set aside to pay for cultural events that are provided free to the community. The banks find it useful in enhancing their visibility and prestige in the community, the government keeps the populace a little happier at no expense to itself, and we all get to go to excellent free concerts, art exhibits, and other cultural activities throughout the year. I suspect they picked up the idea from the Romans, who ruled in Seville a couple of thousand years ago using their famous bread-and-circuses approach to appeasing the citizenry. Nice to know the classics can still teach us something.

I was delighted to find out about these public entertainment options, because we had no TV and, for the first time in my life, I didn't have a steady supply of books to read.

Just typing those last words makes my heart stutter. I've always been a voracious reader, devouring at least a novel or two every week when I'm not on a deadline that cuts down on my reading time. To me, the idea of running out of books was only slightly less frightening than running out of food or air. I'd shipped a huge box of paperbacks to our new apartment, but obviously those wouldn't last me for long. This was just before the advent of e-readers, when Kindle wasn't even a gleam in Amazon's eye, so I needed to figure out how to acquire actual books. I was already familiar with the larger Seville bookstores that carried some English titles, but they cost around seventeen euros (twenty-five dollars) apiece and leaned heavily toward Dan Brown and the gushier British romance novels — not what I wanted as a steady literary diet. I'd heard that Seville had a large library just a twenty-minute walk from our apartment, so I set out one morning to check it out.

The library was a large, modern building tucked in among the trees of the vast Maria Luisa Park. It had acres of bookshelves, but sadly, they held only a paltry supply of books, most of which looked like outcasts from private collections: dog-eared mysteries, popular novels several generations out of date, and obscure nonfiction titles that were probably written by the former owner's great-uncle. There were two shelves of English-language volumes, mostly by Agatha Christie. I love Agatha Christie, but she's not an ideal candidate for rereading; knowing who did it at the outset kind of takes the challenge out of the puzzle.

I managed to find an English mystery written in the 1950s by an unknown author and a Spanish book I thought would help with my reading practice. I soon returned them half-read. For a while I went back regularly to seek other books, hoping each time to find works that weren't quite so lackluster, but the choices only grew more disappointing. Then one day I returned a book a week late and was reaching for my wallet to pay the fine when the librarian explained, more in sorrow than in anger, that the penalty for such a transgression was having my library card suspended for three weeks. I was shocked and mortified. To me, being banned from a library was like hearing the tribe had voted to abandon me on the hillside for the wolves. I slunk away, feeling like an outcast and a criminal, and never returned.

I went back to buying books at the local shops and ordering them by mail from a British-run store down on the coast. Meanwhile, I was checking out other forms of entertainment. Most movie houses ran only dubbed versions of films, which we'd go to occasionally to practice our Spanish; but one did offer films in their original language, and we went about once a week to see the latest Hollywood epic. We had decided not to get a TV, preferring to avoid the parade of garish game shows, infotainment news, and commercial-laden sitcoms available on Spanish channels. Frustratingly, we discovered that Netflix and other online options were accessible only in the United States; no doubt there was some sort of trade agreement, and we could only hope that a policy change would be forthcoming.

Luckily, we could play DVDs on our computer and began renting them locally, simply switching the language track from dubbed Spanish back to the original English. There was a tiny video rental place off Plaza Alfalfa, and we were soon on a first-name basis with the owner, Pepe. Unfortunately, Pepe's selection of DVDs wasn't all that much better than the public library's offerings. We started taking out old favorites; you'd be surprised how many times you can enjoy watching *Ben Hur* and *Breakfast at Tiffany's*.

With such modest home entertainment options, Rich and I were more motivated than ever to go out in the evenings, and we took to frequenting some of the city's many flamenco bars. I love flamenco: the delicate guitar, the wailing cadence of the singer, the haughty glare and sinuous grace of the dancer, the air of glorious, tomorrow-be-damned exuberance. Although few of my Sevillano friends are aficionados, they're all proud of "their" contribution to the world's great music.

While the origins of flamenco remain murky, it's generally agreed that it draws on both gypsy culture and the local folk dance known as the sevillanas, making it uniquely Andalucían in character. In the old days, flamenco was about as racy as entertainment got, with bold women lifting their skirts — above their knees! — and rolling their hips in such suggestive moves that an outraged Franco outlawed flamenco and did his best to repress the gypsy culture altogether. But in the two thousand years that gypsies have been abroad in the world, they've become adept at going underground. No mere law could keep them from singing and dancing and lifting their skirts — they just found more clandestine venues for doing so.

When Franco died in 1975, the popularity of flamenco exploded and public performances sprang up everywhere in Andalucía, especially in Seville. The city is full of flamenco schools and fans, and even the touristy dinner-show places offer good quality performances. I like to go to the small, back-street flamenco bars, where students come to watch their teachers dance and occasionally are invited to jump up on stage and show their moves.

Flamenco is known for its spontaneity, passion, and transformative energy. My French friend Simone was recently at a cooking class when the students discovered that one of their members, a pudgy, mousy little guy, had once danced flamenco. Someone put flamenco music on his iPhone, and everyone begged the former dancer to show what he could do. He demurred for a while but finally agreed.

"It was the most amazing thing," Simone told me. "Here is this guy who is like a snail, all curled in on himself. Suddenly his spine is straight, and his butt, which was very flabby, is now like this!" She held out her hands side by side and clenched them into fists. "Suddenly he has hair — I never noticed he had hair before! He had hair, he had muscles, he had a butt! And he danced. Just a few steps. It was amazing. And then he let it all go, and he became a little snail again. With a pudgy butt."

Flamenco turns up in all sorts of unexpected places, and Rich and I were once lucky enough to be invited to a flamenco wedding. It was held in the chapel at the University of Seville, which was the Royal Tobacco Factory from 1728 to 1950. Back in the day, the *cigarreras* — gypsies and other wild women who defied tradition to work outside the home — rolled cigars on their thighs and gave the factory a pretty outrageous reputation, but now it's a city landmark, and the chapel is the site of many weddings. The one we attended was a full mass with all the trimmings, quite sedate except for the enlivening touch of guitarists playing flamenco tunes instead of hymns.

Rich and I are not very musically inclined, but the free performances sponsored by the banks drew us to the cathedral one night for Handel's *Messiah*. The music and the acoustics were superb, but during the quieter parts I kept hearing a banging sound in the background. I later learned that after the concert's four hundred seats were filled, more than a thousand Sevillanos gathered outside the building, pounding on the cathedral's huge doors with their fists, demanding to be let in. I could not imagine a US crowd in a near riot over classical music. Tickets to Lady Gaga or the Rolling Stones? Sure. Seventeenth-century Baroque composers? Not hardly.

I was loving the way Seville honored the past, but I didn't want to lose all touch with the contemporary cultural mainstream, so I spent a fair amount of time keeping up with current events on the Internet. I watched both American and international news, which often provided startling contrasts in content and perspective. And I exchanged emails with family and friends on a regular basis, so I had a steady supply of everybody's personal news and photos of the kids and grandkids.

I did miss the long, rambling phone chats I used to have with my sisters, sitting in my Ohio kitchen, catching them at home in California, exchanging the small news of the moment. Such calls would have been prohibitively expensive on the pay-as-you-go cell phones that were all we used in Seville. Once in a while I'd go down to an Internet café that offered low-cost long-distance phone calls, where I'd sit on a hard bench in a little white wooden booth with low walls that offered the illusion of privacy while allowing everyone to listen in on each other's calls. It did *not* encourage excessively intimate conversations, and while it was better than nothing, I didn't find it very satisfactory.

Today, Internet-based Skype makes it easy to call anywhere in the world, complete with video if you like, right from the comfort of home. Calls are very low cost, and they're free between Skype users. But that requires both parties being on their computer, so instead of spontaneous calls, I usually schedule Skype sessions in advance. The calls I make are less frequent but longer, often lasting an hour or so.

Others have very different phone connections to home and family. My young American friend Lindsay, who was used to chatting with her mother several times a day while living in the US, now has a Seville cell phone with a calling plan that lets her stay in equally frequent contact every day. They're currently organizing Lindsay's wedding, using Skype calls for major planning sessions, a website to share the latest details with family and friends, and the cell phone to connect throughout the day, with occasional Facebook postings to fill in any gaps.

Our Spanish friend Luz seemed surprised that we didn't maintain that kind of close contact with our families. In fact, she was dumbfounded that we chose to live in Seville at all. Why would we want to be apart from our relatives for anything more than a brief vacation?

I explained that leaving home is an essential part of our heritage. Except perhaps for a few Native Americans, *everyone* in the US comes from broken families. Our ancestors either chose or were forced to leave their loved ones behind to begin a new life in the New World. My own forebears are fairly typical, leaving England, Ireland, and Germany (and probably a few other places) to arrive on the East Coast of the US in the mid-nineteenth century, some later moving on to homestead in the Midwest, with their grown children later traveling by covered wagon to California to seek their fortunes. At each stop along the way, those traveling on had to leave behind relatives who couldn't or wouldn't pull up stakes yet again.

Like most Americans, I grew up thinking it's normal — admirable, even — to move thousands of miles across the country to go to college or take a job or just for a change of pace. As a child I'd lived in California, Virginia, and Connecticut; as an adult I'd added Massachusetts and Ohio to the list. I was accustomed to living apart from my relatives, but now I was doing it in Spain rather than in Cleveland.

Luz and Toño, and later other Spanish friends, weren't buying any of it. Their families had lived in Seville since Hercules was a boy, and they could not conceive of a life that didn't include a circle of friends and relatives that would surround them from cradle to grave. To them, moving on represented not freedom, but loss.

However you look at it, the footloose American lifestyle that brought me to Seville also made me adept at the art of settling into a new environment. And it taught me a lot about the truly important business of making *amigos.*

Chapter 6

MAKING AMIGOS

❧

Moving to a foreign city is an opportunity to reinvent yourself that rarely exists outside of the witness protection program. You get to hit the reset button on your life. Of course, you don't jettison your real baggage; you'll still be carrying around your childhood traumas, the twin hobgoblins of regret and remorse, and all the rest of your deep inner past wherever you go. But you do get to expunge your social record. No one will know anything about you except what you choose to reveal.

Have you ever noticed how the people you grew up with always seem to have the longest memories about the things you'd most like them to forget: ill-chosen hairstyles, undesirable boyfriends, weight fluctuations, foolish business ventures, certain weekends in college? I grew up longing to write fiction, and in my youth I made the mistake of telling people I was working on a novel. I finally realized that nonfiction was my forte and that my efforts at fiction were best consigned to a bottom drawer preceding a trip to the trash bin. But for decades afterwards, well-meaning acquaintances kept cornering me at parties to ask how my novel was coming along. And I'd have to find a cheerful way of explaining that it was an unmitigated disaster that forced me to abandon one of my most cherished childhood dreams. Kind of a buzz-kill, any way you put it.

Moving to a foreign city means never having to say, "Oh yes, my crummy unpublished novel..." It also reduces to virtually nil the chances of running into people from the past you'd rather avoid: ex-bosses, former lovers, people who witnessed your most humiliating moments in high school.

When you are so new in town that your entire social circle consists of a handful of people, it's actually thrilling to spot a familiar face in the crowd. Actually, in Seville, most people treat every chance encounter with the excitement of Stanley greeting Livingstone, exclaiming with surprise and pleasure at the astonishing good luck of running into you. Then everybody kisses each other on the cheeks (right first, then left), unless it's two men, in which case they engage in a firm handshake or, in the case of close friends and family members, a manly hug.

Kisses are dispensed freely, to newly met friends of friends, your hairdresser, neighbors, waiters, or bankers with whom you have built a relationship — pretty much everybody you know by name, unless it's a very strict business relationship, such as the bureaucrats handling residency visas. By now, this deeply entrenched Spanish social ritual has become so automatic to me that I find it's difficult to stop when I'm in the States. I do make an effort to restrain myself, however, since I have found that there, kissing chance-met acquaintances generally results in confusion and alarm; they can't decide whether I'm coming on to them, have become pretentiously European, or am simply losing my mind and believe them to be someone else altogether.

When we arrived in Seville, the first people Rich and I were on kissing terms with were Luz and Toño. I am still astonished at my good fortune in meeting them. Unlike most Sevillanos, they engage with foreigners on a regular basis due to Luz's tourist apartments, and even more unusually, they seem to find them good company. The four of us soon discovered we shared a similar sense of humor and an endless delight in exploring the city's most ancient places, with Toño providing a running commentary on their history.

I loved those excursions, but I have to admit that in the beginning, Toño was one of my more daunting linguistic challenges, a lawyer whose rapid-fire delivery made whole paragraphs flow together like a single word. Having spent his entire life in Seville, Toño knew every inch of its geography and every detail of its long and colorful past. Although he could be serious when discussing such important topics as the city's Roman era or the fifteen-hundred-figure Nativity scene he put up in his guest room every Christmas, Toño generally had a lighthearted and whimsical nature. In fact, his charming insouciance and devil-may-care attitude often made him oblivious to the world around him, and we soon learned he was terrifyingly accident-prone.

Just two years before I met him, when the apartment we rented from Luz was being renovated, Toño was chatting with her when he casually stepped backwards through a window opening and fell three stories to the pavement below. By a miracle he wasn't killed, and after a month or two in the hospital he recovered almost completely. Not long after we met him, he was walking through a construction site and a plank shifted under his weight, sending him tumbling five feet down into a manhole, banging his arms and face bloody. On one visit to the country, I watched in horror as Toño bent over to pet a puppy in a field, oblivious to the fact that a bull was charging toward him; the combined screams of his friends finally alerted him in time to slip out the gate just ahead of the oncoming horns. Once, while taking a shower in another of their rental apartments, Toño fell through the glass shower door, cutting his face rather badly; however, since that particular apartment is said to be haunted, some claim he was pushed by the ghost and maintain that this accident can't reasonably be held to be his fault.

I soon learned that during our excursions, it was everyone's job to grab Toño's arm and pull him out of the path of oncoming traffic. His long, rambling tours took us through the city's narrow back streets, across its great boulevard and plazas, and deep into obscure palaces, half-forgotten churches, and ancient convents. We'd amble through ancient patios drowsing in the sun to visit dark chambers where wizened nuns guarded treasures their long-ago sisters had brought to the church as a dowry. One of my favorites was a nail from the True Cross, although I have seen quite a few of these on display throughout Europe; apparently there were hundreds of these nails holding up the Savior.

The first time that Luz and Toño invited us to join a small group for dinner at their apartment, I was thrilled. I'd been told repeatedly that the Spanish do all their entertaining in restaurants and cafés, and that I should resign myself to the fact that I would never see the inside of a Spanish home. True, Rich and I had attended cooking classes in the apartment of our teacher, Yolanda, but this was the first time we were visiting someone's home for purely social purposes.

We arrived on their doorstep in our best clothes, carrying wine and flowers. Luz was far too polite to say anything, but we soon learned that in Seville, the proper hostess gift is nearly always a dessert, preferably something laden with whipped cream. Luz introduced us to the other guests, a small group that included her sister, Violeta, who was older, taller, blonder, and if possible, even more exquisitely groomed than Luz herself; and Toño's brother, Marco, who had sleepy, long-lashed eyes and something of a reputation as a *golfo* (playboy). As the frothy sweets others had brought were being passed around, Luz turned to me and asked, "How do you feel about bullfights?"

I thought they were about as much fun as seeing one of my beloved dogs thrown into a ring and tortured to death as a public spectacle. However, feeling a more tactful reply was called for, I said that while I naturally respected their place in the Spanish culture and admired their artistry, I found them difficult to watch because I had sympathy for the bull.

She nodded as if this was the answer she expected. "How would you like to go to a *capea*, a private bullfight that's done for practice, where they don't kill the bull? You can experience part of our culture; I think it would be interesting for you."

A definite yes! We made arrangements to meet on Saturday and drive out to a big farm near the Portuguese border where the *capea* would be taking place.

After many hours of driving, getting repeatedly lost, and course correcting without either a map or GPS to guide us, we somehow, eventually, arrived at the farm. Parking on the side of the road, we began walking up the long driveway.

Almost immediately a forklift came trundling toward us, carrying the corpse of a huge black bull, head lolling, blood dripping everywhere, with a one-eyed white pit bull running along beside it, trying to lick the blood off the bull's face.

"I think they're killing the *toros* today!" I whispered to Rich in dismay.

But it was too late to turn back now. Luz asked the forklift driver what was going on, and we learned that some apprentice bullfighters from northern Mexico and the American Southwest were there to test themselves in the ring, fighting live bulls for the first time and killing them if possible. They had no doubt paid handsomely for the use of the ring and for the six young bulls that would die that day. For even if a *torero* (the preferred Spanish term for bullfighter) failed to finish off his opponent, the bulls were ruined for the ring and would be slaughtered and eaten.

Although this was meant to be a strictly private affair, the group seemed delighted to add us to their small audience and pressed us to stay for the bullfight and for lunch; we could see men setting enormous paella pans on two outdoor grills. Luz assumed that Rich had a manly interest in blood sports but asked me if I wanted to stay. I did. I may not be a big fan of ritual animal slaughter in a general way, but this was a rare opportunity to witness something special in the Sevillano culture, and I wasn't about to miss it. Besides, after the long drive, I knew my companions, including Rich, would *not* be pleased to turn around and leave now. Let the games begin.

Someone from the farm led us up a long metal staircase and across a catwalk to a tiny viewing stand. Crossing the catwalk, I looked down to see that it spanned a pair of pens holding young bulls that were snorting and shifting about restlessly, jostling each other and pawing the ground with their hooves. I bent over for a closer look until somebody said, "Don't get too close. Bulls can jump like cats." Yikes! An important safety tip! I stood upright in a hurry and walked briskly along to the safety of the viewing platform.

I have been to bullfights before and since, but watching these amateurs taking their (literally) first stab at it, it actually felt like something close to a fair fight. It wasn't, of course. The game is well and truly stacked in the humans' favor. Every *torero's* support team, or *cuadrilla*, includes a *picador*, who rides in on a heavily padded horse and stabs a short lance into the bull's neck, weakening the muscle so the bull can't raise its head properly. After that, several *banderilleros* run in on foot to jab beribboned spikes into the bull's neck to further harass the animal. At this point the *torero* engages the bull, using his cape to first excite, then control, and finally subdue the beast until he can get close enough to stick a sword straight down through its neck into its heart.

It's a grisly process. But I have to admit that when done well, it's a magnificent display of human courage, skill, and grace. It's easy to see why the Spanish view it as an art form and why the newspapers cover it in the culture section, not sports.

Done badly, it's pure butchery. Rich and I once went to a bullfight in a small town in Mexico, where we were seated so close to the barrier that I kept looking down to see if any of the blood was getting on my shoes. And there was a lot of blood. The first two *matadores* (as the Mexicans prefer to call them) seemed clumsy, even to my untutored eye, and the third was having an especially bad day and simply could not finish off the bull. The poor beast had been poked and pierced by the *picador* and the *banderilleros*, then chased around the ring and stabbed repeatedly by the *matador*, but it was still standing, sides heaving, glaring malevolently at its attacker. The *matador* was red-faced and seething with frustration.

As the grisly fiasco wore on, I grew more and more tense. I didn't want the bull to be killed at all, but if it had to happen, I wanted the *torero* to get on with it and finish the job cleanly.

None of the people around me seemed to share my distress. It was Easter Sunday, and the stands were crowded with families, from ancient grandmothers to wriggling toddlers, all eating roasted peanuts sprinkled with salt and lime juice, shouting encouragement to the *matador* and keeping up a running commentary on the fight's progress. Our neighbors watched us out of the corners of their eyes and seemed amused at my appalled reaction to the blood-soaked spectacle.

The *matador* made another abortive attempt to jam his sword between the beast's shoulder blades, but the bull lumbered aside just in time, the blow glancing off, leaving a new gouge in its already bleeding shoulder. The *matador* hopped about, nearly apoplectic with rage.

"He is losing it," I said to Rich. "This is when mistakes happen."

The words were scarcely out of my mouth when the bull got its horns under the backside of the *matador* and flung him into the air. The man landed practically at our feet, blood pouring from his nether regions. For one horrified moment I thought he was dead. The crowd erupted to their feet with a roar of excitement.

Some of the bullring staff ran out with guns, ready to shoot the bull, but the *matador* managed to lurch to his knees and wave them away. He was going to finish this himself, never mind that the seat of his pants was flapping in the breeze and his blood was dripping steadily onto the sandy ground. The clamor of the crowd died down as he rose unsteadily to his feet. I held my breath.

The *matador* staggered forward, members of his *cuadrilla* ran to join him, and together they forced the bull against the wall. The *matador* started jabbing his sword into the bull's neck, over and over again. There was no skill, just violence. I felt sick to my stomach. I couldn't stand to watch, and I couldn't look away. With the crowd shouting encouragement and jeers, the *matador* kept up his brutal attack, and after what seemed an eternity, the bull finally fell to its knees, collapsed, and died. Only then did the *matador* let his own knees buckle; he sank to the ground, unconscious, and was rushed away for medical attention.

"Okay, that's about all the fun I can take in one afternoon," I said to Rich. He nodded, looking almost as shaken as I felt.

We stood up and walked out, the crowd around us grinning and poking each other in the ribs and giving each other little I-told-you-so eye rolls. These *gringos*. What a bunch of wimps.

I realized they felt the way I would if I went to a football game or hockey match and saw some effete foreigner stomp out over the unnecessary roughness of play. Hey, whaddaya want, this is a contact sport! But I was beyond caring what anyone thought of me. I just wanted out.

And I wasn't the only one. Leaving the bullring and climbing into one of the small vans used for public transportation, I recognized the half-dozen other foreigners who'd been at the bullfight, all of us looking slightly sheepish, rather green about the gills, and anxious to get away from the gruesome spectacle.

We didn't get that much blood or drama at the *capea* on the Portuguese border. But the bulls were young and feisty, and the *toreros* were inexperienced and, in some cases, hampered by bodies that were no longer young or agile. There were a lot of mad dashes for the protective barriers along the wall, and several of the slower *toreros* were knocked down and trampled. None of the men seemed seriously hurt. In fact, the person whose life appeared most at risk was one portly, middle-aged fellow who, while leaning up against the wall waiting his turn in the ring, was wheezing so badly that I kept mentally rehearsing CPR protocols.

I could tell it was a peak moment for him and the other first-timers, all of whom had spent years practicing for this day, culminating in a week working with a retired Spanish bullfighter of some fame. The bullfighter stood as straight as a *picador*'s lance at the edge of the ring, watching his students with a critical eye. Many of them showed up in gaudy outfits that looked more like mariachi costumes than the traditional Spanish "suit of lights." It would have been easy to think of them as slightly desperate and absurd wannabes, like Billy Crystal's character in *City Slickers*. But I had to admire their courage when they were standing alone in the ring, face to face with a furious thousand-pound bull that knew it was fighting for its life.

After we watched two *toreros* kill their bulls with what seemed to me a reasonable degree of amateur skill, Luz suggested we take a break. We headed down the stairs just in time to watch one of the recently dispatched bulls being hoisted up by its hind feet on a pulley. Before I could say "Do I really want to see this?" one of the men was skinning it, cutting up the flesh, and throwing chunks of it on the barbeque. The next thing I knew, someone handed me a plate of sizzling chunks of grilled bull meat and a fork.

Having just watched this animal fighting for its life, the sight of its seared flesh sitting on my plate made me feel a bit queasy, almost like a cannibal. I had to remind myself sternly that this was the way humans had been eating since the dawn of time (or at least since the dawn of fire and cooking). Besides, to turn up my nose at food offered in kindness would offend both the cooks and the friends who brought me. Part of belonging to any community is joining in the communal feast, and I knew that I was lucky to be offered the chance. I took a bite of the bull meat. It was hot and salty and delicious. In fact, washed down with the crisp local beer, it was superb.

As usual, saying yes to one of Luz's invitations had proved to be a great idea. But a few weeks later, when she suggested that I join her art class, I tried to say no. I felt I was learning about as many new things as my brain could process without imploding.

"It doesn't matter whether or not you want to learn art," Luz explained. "It's a great way to meet people. It will be good for your social life." Well, when she put it that way, how could I resist?

Every Wednesday afternoon, Luz picked me up and we drove twenty minutes outside the city to the small town where her sister lived. The class was subsidized by the local government and held in a small rented storefront that barely had room for the fifteen or so students, mostly Spanish matrons in their forties and fifties. The teacher, Ricardo, was a handsome, amiable man who never made much of an attempt to teach us anything. He had long ago realized that his character wasn't strong enough to stand up to the dynamic personalities in his class, especially Luz and her sister Violeta. Both were vibrant women with kind and generous hearts, keen intelligence, and tremendous natural leadership ability, and when something needed to be done, they never hesitated to step forward. My first day of class coincided with a move to new quarters, and Ricardo had arrived early to arrange the easels and chairs. Violeta walked in, took one look, and said, "This won't do at all!" She proceeded to rearrange the room, improving the configuration immensely but doing nothing for Ricardo's self-esteem.

Everybody then sat down at an easel and began to copy the works of other artists, such as the *Mona Lisa* and Van Gogh's sunflowers. From time to time Ricardo would wander over, take the brush out of someone's hand, and begin correcting the painting — an intrusion into the artistic process that would have been a hanging offense in most serious art studios in the US. But in this class, painting was as much craft as art, more about following the lead of proven geniuses than striking out on your own creative journey.

I gradually got to know my fellow art students, among them a nurse, a baker, a musician, a teacher, a hotelier who had worked in Germany and had a German husband, several housewives, and a rather fragile man in his seventies who liked to live up to his reputation as a *golfo* by painting nude women. All of them were extremely kind and patient with me, explaining techniques and repeating the choicer bits of news and gossip more slowly to make sure I didn't miss them.

This was one group of Spanish friends that hadn't known each other since birth, which meant it was a great deal easier for me to become a part of it. Of course, as a foreigner, I would always be the odd one out, practically the class mascot, and we all knew it. But being introduced to them as Luz's friend meant that a little of her high social status rubbed off on me, and they made every effort to overlook my strangeness and incorporate me into their circle. I enjoyed their company and felt lucky to be there, and I made sure I showed it.

Luz was right; the class was wonderful for my social life. Every session included a break for coffee, cake, and chitchat, and every couple of months Ricardo organized an excursion to a museum or gallery, outings that included our spouses and inevitably ended up in a café for beer and tapas. Actually, Ricardo's role in organizing these outings was primarily that of wielding a rubber stamp; Luz and Violeta came up with the ideas, did all the planning, and made all the phone calls.

Not long after I joined the class, the sisters made arrangements for all the painters and their partners to spend a weekend away at a place their brother owned in the country. He had converted an old windmill into a vacation rental that reflected his own avant-garde attitude toward privacy: he didn't hold with it. Each room opened up on every other room, so there was little visual separation and no barrier at all against the myriad snores and rustlings and trips to the bathroom that two dozen middle-aged people can make in the night. There was one conventional bathroom in the main house, plus an outbuilding designed by the brother with four showers on one side and four toilets on the other, where men and women were meant to commingle freely. It was much like today's college dorms or the old hippie crash pads of my youth.

The weekend was a sort of symphony of outside-my-comfort-zone experiences. At Sunday afternoon's barbeque, the sisters suddenly asked me to sing an American song to entertain the group. I am *not* a singer, and for a second I half expected to look down, notice I was naked, and think, "Well, thank God, it's only a nightmare." But it was real life, and I could not refuse without appearing exceedingly ungracious. My heart pounded, my palms began to sweat, and my mind went blank. Did I even know the words to any songs? Of course I did. And Rich was there to support me, although as you'll no doubt recall, he is not exactly a musical virtuoso, especially without his triangle. In the end, we belted out a version of "For He's a Jolly Good Fellow" with more volume than artistry, and everyone kindly applauded the effort and told us we should keep our day jobs. Someone videotaped the performance and gave me a DVD copy, but I've never been able to bring myself to watch it. Some parts of your past are better left in the rearview mirror.

I was beginning to feel the same way about our life in Cleveland. After six months in Spain, it was hard to imagine going back there for any extended amount of time. I felt so much more vital and alive when I was in Seville, so energized and excited. Returning to Ohio began to seem like going home to live with your parents after college, a capitulation to expediency that would mark the end of a grand adventure. I didn't want my adventuring days to telescope down to a few weeks of vacation a year. Rich and I began discussing a second year in Seville, and it didn't take us long to decide we would renew our lease and our tourist visas and stay on.

We sent a flurry of emails off to the States notifying our friends and family, who seemed less surprised than we were by this development. As one California friend put it, "Seville or Cleveland? Was there ever really a question?"

We flew back to Ohio to check on the house, make the rounds of our doctors and dentists, sign a few papers with our financial people, and visit with family and those friends who were still speaking to us. For the first year away we'd hired a house sitter, but now we rented the house to a neighbor going through a divorce. We knew this would please Luz; it had offended her landlady's soul to think we were paying money for someone to stay in what should be an income-producing property.

Returning for our second year in Seville, I signed up for more art classes, and I was really enjoying them until the day that Ricardo went postal on us.

At the time I was working on the largest piece I'd ever attempted, a roughly three-by-five-foot painting of a weathered eighteenth-century church. I was struggling with the architectural perspective and asked Ricardo for help with the angle of a roofline that didn't look quite right to me. His suggestion was so clearly wrong that I hesitated, drew Violeta and some of the others into the discussion, and finally ignored his advice to go with the recommendation of the group. This happened all the time in his classes. We all felt free to override his suggestions and paint over his corrections; several others had already done so that day. Ricardo usually ignored the insult with a shrug and a smile, but today, from the moment he entered the classroom, he made it clear he was tired of feeling like a second-class citizen in his own art studio. He was striking back.

Since we were in Spain instead of America, his going postal didn't involve pulling out a gun and shooting anybody. Instead, he went through an emotional breakdown that lasted the entire three hours of the class. Normally the most mild-mannered of men, that day he started out snippy, moved on to hostile, progressed to tearful fury, and ended with kicking Luz and Violeta out of the class altogether. I remember standing there with my paintbrush, working on the roofline of the church, while all about me emotionally charged Spanish was flying about the room. Was I hearing this right? What did he mean, he had nothing more to teach Luz and Violeta? Was he really telling them, and those of us who were their friends, to get out and not come back?

Afterwards, shell-shocked, we all stumbled to the café down the block to try to sort out what had just happened. On the way Luz said bitterly, "Violeta and I drove him to his hemorrhoidectomy last month. And this is how he repays us?!"

The group would speak of The Incident for years, hashing over every nuance of each disparaging remark, trying to make sense of the outburst. It was generally agreed Ricardo had emotional problems and was taking them out on us.

Meanwhile, we had to find another art teacher. Naturally the task fell to the sisters, and Luz eventually contacted Margarita, an art professor from whom she'd taken classes ten years earlier. By now Margarita was well into her seventies, an impatient old woman with poor eyesight who had been teaching people to copy the same art prints for decades, possibly generations. Painting sessions were held in a cramped, poorly ventilated classroom in a high school that was kept under perpetual lockdown in a barrio an hour away by bus, on the edge of the one seriously scary and dangerous neighborhood in the province. The first thing I was told was never, ever to use the school bathrooms; I never did find out why, and it was probably best left that way. There was electricity in the classroom but not in the hall or on the stairs, which we stumbled down in the pitch dark after class, lugging wet paintings and huge tote bags filled with art supplies.

Margarita put us to work copying faded, dog-eared prints of obscure paintings while she chain-smoked in the corner. Here, even more than in Ricardo's class, the goal was conformity rather than creativity. Margarita told us exactly what colors and techniques to use and insisted on approving each phase of our work before we could continue to the next. Often she'd approve something, then later come along and announce it was all wrong and must be rubbed off with turpentine and started again. I spent three months painting a pot of geraniums over and over, under conflicting directions, without any discernable improvement. I finally realized I wasn't supposed to be reproducing the original print, I was supposed to be reproducing her *interpretation* of the original print, leaving out details she was too shortsighted to see and pumping up the colors that were too dim for her fading vision. As I attempted to guess what she wanted, she would stand behind me shouting, "Coward! Coward! Don't be so afraid. Paint! Paint!"

After one such frustrating session, I stumbled down the dark stairs and out into the rainy evening, following the group to the nearest café for a restorative decaf coffee before we went our separate ways. I felt windblown and frustrated and out of sorts as we settled down with our drinks.

Out of the blue, Violeta said to me, "Where do you get your hair done?"

I looked at her blankly, not sure I was hearing her correctly. Why was she asking about *that?*

"My sister told me not to mention this," she went on. Luz stared hard at her sister, and the others shifted uncomfortably in their chairs and looked away, clearly knowing what was coming. "But I need to talk to you about your hair."

"My *hair?*" I'd arrived in Seville with one of those short, boyish cuts that are so delightfully effortless to maintain. Then, having observed that my local friends strongly favored long, layered, curling hair with blond streaks, I began letting my hair grow and even experimented a bit with highlights, although the blonder tones looked awful on me and I soon stopped doing it. I finally found a hairdresser who understood that I wanted a sleek, natural look in my own hair color (or what had been my own hair color, before the ravages of time), and I felt that my coiffure was looking the best it had in years.

"My *hair?*" I repeated. "I go to a little salon downtown, near El Corte Inglés. Why?"

"We have all talked about it. And we've decided that your hair is too serious."

At first I couldn't take it in. It was an *intervention.* About my *hair.*

"Don't you want hair that is happier?" she went on. "You could make it more blonde, give it some curls..."

Violeta wanted me to look more like them. I didn't have the heart to tell her that where I come from, their hairstyles hadn't been popular since Farrah Fawcett Majors left the original cast of

Charlie's Angels. Although the elaborate styles looked perfect in the context of Seville, if I showed up in California with that kind of big, fluffy, streaked hair, everyone would assume I'd taken up a career as either a country and western singer or a hooker.

"Violeta," I began. "Hair styles are different in different cultures..."

Luckily, at that moment, just when it seemed the conversation might turn awkward, a sewer full of rainwater overflowed near our feet, flooding the café and making us all snatch up our art supplies and rush for the door. In the ensuing confusion, the subject was dropped and never raised again.

I stuck it out in Margarita's class for quite a while, but when others began dropping out, eventually I did too. If I was going to risk my life in the barrio and on the stairs (to say nothing of the bathrooms), I wanted to do it for something more worthwhile than producing my own amateurish copies of undistinguished art.

I began painting at home, which was far more satisfactory, but I was concerned about losing contact with the women in my art class. I was accepted as a member of the group, even if I was a foreigner with serious hair, but I was not on terms of intimate friendship with anyone but Luz. If I bumped into one of my classmates on the street, we'd talk, maybe even go for coffee, but we didn't call each other up for one-on-one lunches or evenings out with our husbands. Once again, Luz and Violeta came to the rescue. No one wanted the group to disband, so the sisters continued to organize excursions, dinners, holiday parties, and movie nights, keeping the group and our collective friendship going.

One day over coffee I was telling the story of the hair intervention to an American friend who has lived in Seville a long time.

"They said I should change my hair because it's too *serious*," I exclaimed.

"They only said that because they love you."

I instantly realized she was right. In the US, unsolicited criticism of someone's hair, weight, or clothing could end a friendship. But here in Seville, where a greater degree of frankness is common and there's a higher priority placed on conformity, I could see it was kindly meant. Violeta and the other women were cluing me in about what I needed to do in order to be one of the gang. The implication that this kind of belonging could be achieved by a mere change in hairstyle made it the loveliest insult I had ever received.

Chapter 7

EXPATS

☙

Every once in a while, I run into fellow expats who make it clear they aren't interested in my friendship, declaring their intent to associate exclusively with Sevillanos because they want the full immersion experience. While this is a laudable goal, and certainly the fastest way to acquire the language and learn the nuances of the culture, most people can't keep it up for long. As I had found hanging out with my art class, conversing in another tongue all the time is exhausting. Curtailing your commentary to fit the limits of your elementary vocabulary is frustrating, as is the lack of a shared cultural context that lets you make sense of each other's jokes and opinions. Most Spanish friendships are built over a lifetime, and as an outsider you'll always be playing catch-up. You'll often find yourself hovering around the fringes rather than joining the inner circle, which can leave you feeling isolated even in a crowd.

These are the facts of expat life that we all have to come to terms with, especially here, in such a traditional society. Even Spaniards arriving from other cities complain of feeling like outsiders in Seville. As a friend from Salamanca put it, "The

Sevillanos welcome you with open arms, but they never actually wrap those arms around you." But then, all friendships have limitations. I have American friends with whom I can't touch on a wide range of subjects without nuclear reprisals. Yet I value our relationship and enjoy their company. I just make sure I have a broad enough social circle to collectively meet the full range of my needs. In Seville, this means a mix of friends from every part of the globe, including Seville and other parts of Spain. I share great times with all of them, but in different ways.

Sooner or later, even the diehards come to this realization. They abandon their attempts to stick it out in full immersion and join the rest of us who actively seek the company of our fellow expats.

And here I should mention for the record that the term "expatriate" or "expat" does not mean we are no longer loyal to our country of origin; it just means we have left our country to live abroad. Rich and I are still patriotic Americans. Yes, we are! We just don't choose to live there all the time.

When we took up residence in Seville, I did an Internet search and turned up a social club that was open to English-speaking women of all nationalities. An email requesting more information resulted in an invitation to their upcoming monthly luncheon at a downtown restaurant. I arrived to find several dozen women hailing from America, England, Ireland, Australia, France, Austria, Germany, Sri Lanka, India, and several other countries, plus a number of Spanish women who had American or British husbands or who simply wanted to practice their language skills. Everyone was drinking wine, tucking into generous plates of food, and talking at once.

I liked the club. It had 140 members and the simple agenda of providing a social life for these women and their families by organizing holiday parties, monthly luncheons, a book club, activities for moms with young kids, and, I was thrilled to learn, a large lending library of books in English.

The club's hard-working directors had all been serving on the board for years, swapping roles around a bit but basically running the show year after year. They were understandably exhausted but hadn't managed to convince anyone to take over for them. Their jobs were more demanding than ever that year, because no one would agree to serve as president and they were all sharing those tasks among themselves.

I had an idea for a new activity, and when I went to talk to the board about it, five minutes into the conversation they offered me the presidency; I think my main qualification was that I was breathing. I turned them down at once. I was happy to help row the boat, but I wasn't ready to grab the helm.

Then I told them about my idea: a welcome committee that would organize nights out for new and potential members, giving them the opportunity to meet in small groups with club veterans. I figured if nothing else, heading up such gatherings would give me a chance to meet lots of people in the expat community. The board approved my proposal and then casually mentioned they were all stepping down at the end of the year, whether or not any replacements came forward. I was dismayed at the idea that my newfound social network could be on the brink of unraveling and wondered if there was anything I could do (short of taking over the presidency) to keep it stitched together a little longer.

As it turned out, launching the welcome committee did the trick. It was an instant success, a series of lively evenings for women and their partners in a popular local tapas bar. By the end of each evening, a lot of newcomers were ready to join the club and volunteer for a committee — often the welcome committee, so that they could keep on having evenings like this. From the welcome committee, it was often just a short step to a board position or some other active role in the club, and more importantly, to the friendships that give life its zip and savor. The club began to revitalize, and Rich and I spent many enjoyable evenings on the town with new arrivals from a wide assortment of countries, backgrounds, and generations.

One of the great things about being an expat in a town with a relatively small foreign population is that you have friends of all ages — in my case, from twenties to eighties. Where most societies are highly stratified along generational lines, our expat community is, of necessity, far more likely to intermingle. With such a small pool to draw upon, when I'm lucky enough to find people whose language, interests, and personality are compatible with mine, I don't really care whether their favorite band of all time is the Beatles, Hootie and the Blowfish, LMFAO, or Guy Lombardo and His Royal Canadians.

Very early on, Rich and I met an engaging young English couple at a club function, and the four of us began having dinner together every week or two, drinking wine and laughing over our common struggles to understand the Spanish and their language. The couple had lived in the Canary Islands and now planned to make a new life for themselves in Seville. I was just settling into the comfortable feeling that this was the beginning of a beautiful friendship when they suddenly announced they were moving back to England. They just didn't feel they could build careers in Spain, and he was thinking of going to medical school, right after he took a motorcycle trip through Iran...

It was a shock. It always is, when a friend suddenly rejects the life you have in common and declares the intention of moving on to bigger and better adventures. I had done the same thing to my friends in Ohio, and I now began to feel a much greater sympathy for their reactions. Taking a cue from my neighbor Nancy, I told the young couple I didn't want them to go, this was obviously a bad decision, but... how could I help?

This was the first of many such losses, and as such, it served as a sort of inoculation that made the later ones easier to bear. In an expat community, people come and go with tremendous frequency for every possible reason. I began to understand why club members who'd lived in Seville for decades were always asking me, "How long do you plan to stay?" Like the *butaneros* who replace the butane tanks, they didn't want to invest in our relationship if I wasn't going to stick around.

When someone interesting arrives in town and appears likely to stay awhile, we actively pass them along to one another the way San Franciscans pass on food recommendations. Instead of "You must try the new Mexican-Indian fusion restaurant in the Mission," people are apt to say, "You must meet Molly, who's just moved here from Dublin." Molly was passed on to me by Christine, a dancer from New Zealand who had given up a position in the Cadbury chocolate testing department (dream job!) to travel around the world studying dance. Christine was passed on to me by Johanna, a Belgian who ran the *Carmen* tour, an English-language guided visit to sites around town that provided the backdrop to Bizet's famous opera. You see how the system works.

So thanks to Johanna, Christine, and the new-girl network, I got to know Molly, a lively, generous, and big-hearted Irishwoman who is always ready to share a laugh over a pint. She'd gone to work for the Bank of Ireland in her youth, and when she discovered that she qualified for early retirement in her forties, she was off like a shot. She chose Seville for the better weather, lower prices, and the Spanish version of "pub culture" — that is, lots of friendly, sociable bars where people gather to watch sporting events.

At the time we met, Molly was going out with Mauri, a slim, good-looking Spaniard ten years her junior. When I suggested the four of us meet up a few nights later at a bar near the Alameda de Hercules, Molly shook her head.

"Mauri can't go to the Alameda."

"Why not?"

"Death threats."

I was sorry for Mauri's troubles, but I have to admit I was secretly thrilled. Hardly anybody I knew back in Cleveland had death threats against them. It was so much more colorful here.

Molly is blessed with keen intelligence, a good sense of humor, and a refreshingly straightforward approach to life. She knows what she loves and goes after it: congenial company, cold beer, good food, Irish rugby, and her dogs. The first of her dogs was Sláinte (pronounced SLAHN-cha), which is the Gaelic toast to your health. When they adopted the pretty little red-gold mutt with big brown eyes, everyone agreed Sláinte had Molly's hair and Mauri's eyes.

There was considerably less agreement about how Sláinte happened to get pregnant. Mauri claimed Molly had left her tied up too long outside the market; Molly was sure it happened when the dog accompanied Mauri to a construction job. Both admitted it would have been better if they had gotten around to taking her in to get spayed before some unknown dog had his way with her. In due course the "puppies of shame" were born, each emerging with such wildly different hair color and body type that we began to wonder how many fathers had been involved. Maybe Molly and Mauri were both right about how the pregnancy occurred.

Eventually, and rather reluctantly, Mauri took Sláinte to the vet for spaying. There he was delighted to learn the surgery could be done in such a way that she could still go into heat and have sex, just not reproduce. Mauri felt his pet would enjoy having a sex life — and she did, as often as possible, as soon as her puppies were weaned and given away. She was very popular. When one of her male puppies was returned, the two dogs soon yielded to their baser instincts and began having prolonged and enthusiastic sex throughout Molly's apartment at all hours of the day and night. This first occurred the week that all Molly's Irish friends and relatives arrived to celebrate her birthday, and the guests kept saying, "Aren't they mother and son? Does anyone share my alarm?"

Although our own dog, Pie, was many years and a successful surgery past her sexually active days, she wasn't lacking for adventure and romance. She and I began every day with a long walk in a large park behind the old royal palace, and there she encountered new friends, one enemy, and the great love of her life.

Unlike our Ohio neighbors, who favored bigger breeds such as Labradors and golden retrievers, most apartment-dwelling Sevillanos owned smaller pets, and Pie had the gratifying sensation of towering over many of her new acquaintances. Maybe it was a size thing, but one miniature Doberman pinscher took an instant dislike to Pie, lunging and snapping and snarling at her whenever he caught sight of her. Pie used to try to pretend the little fellow was beneath her notice while at the same time scurrying behind my legs for protection.

One day she met an elderly chocolate Lab named Bruno, who was one of the homeliest dogs I've ever seen. But underneath that underwhelming exterior, he evidently possessed some inner quality that made Pie's heart beat faster. The two of them took one look at each other, made a few brief, delicate overtures, and began to frolic like puppies. I found it heartbreakingly sweet to see these two aged dogs gamboling about in the early morning sun, eyes alight with the sheer pleasure of each other's company. After that, I made a special effort to get to the park when Bruno and his owner liked to take their morning walk. Unfortunately, this meant getting up twenty minutes earlier every day, but who was I to stand in the way of true love? Whenever we did manage to catch up with Bruno, it was a red-letter day for Pie.

So Pie's social life was the best it had been in years, maybe ever, and mine was on the upswing too. In the fall of our second year in Seville, I took on the job of vice president of the women's club and persuaded Molly to become the club's treasurer. My main task was organizing holiday parties and special events, and the two of us spent many happy hours checking out local bars and restaurants as possible venues. Molly was proving to be the kind of dependable pal you could count on to lend a hand with any enterprise. When we saw that another club friend, Carol, was overwhelmed by the task of clearing out the apartment of an American woman who'd passed away, Molly and I volunteered to help.

It was a grim task. The American woman had died by her own hand after a long and painful bout of cancer. She had lived for many years in the heart of old Seville, in a tiny two-bedroom apartment that was jammed, floor to ceiling, with stuff. I have never seen such a pack rat. There were clothes reflecting fashions and weight changes spanning decades, a lot of the pieces in pristine condition with price tags still attached. She had a drawer full of gorgeous, expensive lingerie; after seeing it, Molly and I both went home and culled our own collections, and I've been making an effort to upgrade ever since. There were hundreds of books, thick with dust and smelling of tobacco and must. The narrow hallway was lined with containers holding dozens of pairs of shoes. The kitchen cupboards were a solid mass of boxes and bins stuffed with gadgets and china. There were tightly packed storage boxes under the bed and even in the shower. And practically every object had a designated recipient.

Before her death, the woman had written instructions that ran on for page after closely typed page. "If Barbara doesn't want the TV, talk to Pablo. If he doesn't want it, ask Maria Luisa. If she can't take it, try..." Very few of these people wanted anything, but Carol dutifully called each and every one, in order, as instructed. The handful who actually showed up would drift sadly through the apartment, collecting a few random books, scarves, and bits of pottery, which they would then pile in the middle of the floor before wandering out again, murmuring vaguely about returning to collect them later, leaving us stepping over depressing little piles of mementos every time we went in or out of the room.

By the end of three weeks, we had managed to give away about 0.01 percent of the designated items. In another week the lease on the apartment would expire, and Carol made the practical decision that the three of us could start taking any of the nondesignated things that we wanted. I carted home a great many books, cartons of kitchenware, and a few really gorgeous skirts. But the apartment was still overflowing as we kept unearthing more and more storage boxes.

One day, as I was digging through a pile of African musical instruments and chipped pottery on the living room windowsill, I came across an object I hadn't previously noticed. I thought at first it was an oversized cocktail shaker with a zippered carrying case, but when I opened it up, I discovered a clean silver container with the name of a funeral home stamped on it. It was the urn that had held the woman's ashes before her brother came from the States to scatter them.

"I didn't want to throw it away," Carol explained. "I thought somebody might want it."

For what? Mixing martinis for the Addams family?

Most of the activities Molly and I undertook were considerably more cheerful, such as organizing the club's welcome committee nights and holiday parties. That year we were in charge of the Christmas fiesta, a rollicking affair held in the back room of a seafood restaurant. Rich invited a new acquaintance of his to join us, a young Englishman known as L-F who had recently moved to Seville with his wife and baby daughter. L-F was a delightful dinner companion, the life and soul of the party, but he refused to tell us anything about his past, his current profession, or even his name, and when someone brought out a camera, he flung a napkin in front of his face to keep from being photographed.

"He must be in the witness protection program," Rich said.

"No, it's probably death threats," I said. "Does he know Mauri?"

Over the next year, Rich and I began seeing a lot of L-F and his brilliant, elegant French wife, Simone. The four of us went out regularly for dinner and philosophical discussions. Someone would always come up with a question, such as "Do you believe in energy healing? If so, how does it work?" Or "What do you fear most about getting old?" Or "What things that are legal now do you think should be illegal, and what illegal things should be legal?" Naturally, the discussions would grow increasingly eloquent and profound as the evening and the beer consumption advanced.

About once a week, Rich and L-F would meet up for a drink and a little quiet conversation at the end of the day. Being fans of the TV program *Boston Legal,* they modeled these evenings on the scene at the end of every show in which the two lawyers, Denny Crane and Alan Shore, sip scotch, puff on cigars, and discuss their day and the meaning of life. Instead of sitting on an executive balcony overlooking the skyline of Boston, L-F and Rich set up folding chairs in a rather scruffy little square known to all (except the cartographers) as Plaza del Pato (Duck Plaza), for the statue that tops the big old stone fountain presiding over one end. The plaza is near the local high school, making it a favorite haunt of youngsters seeking a quiet place for drinking or courting, and features a gypsy-owned bar that attracts a variety of colorful characters.

Late one blazing hot night, I was returning home from a club meeting and passed through Duck Plaza to find Rich and L-F sitting in folding chairs with their feet up on the rim of the duck fountain, sipping scotch from a little silver flask. Although their *Boston Legal* nights were usually sacrosanct, on this occasion they generously invited me to join them and passed me the flask. Rich came to sit beside me on the edge of the fountain. After a while, we took off our shoes and began dipping our toes in the cool water. Then Rich planted his feet in the fountain and stood up.

"Come on in," he said. "The water feels great."

I slipped off the cool stone into the cooler water and took a few steps, wading in water up to my knees.

"God, it's wonderful," I said.

Rich, who can never resist a movie moment, swept me into his arms and began to waltz me around. I felt dizzy and romantic all at the same time, laughing in Rich's arms as we danced around the fountain. I thought we made a much better showing than

Marcello Mastroianni and Anita Ekberg, who mostly just waded about in the famous Trevi Fountain scene in *La Dolce Vita.*

Then an old man passing by growled at us, "Hey you two, is that any way to behave?"

I froze, instantly transformed from Anita Ekberg to Dennis the Menace.

But Rich just laughed. "Relax," he murmured in my ear. "I read somewhere that once the temperature gets this high, it's actually legal to get into the fountains to cool off."

Evidently the old curmudgeon wasn't familiar with that piece of legislation, because as he crossed to the far side of the plaza he half turned to growl back at us over his shoulder, "You wouldn't do that back where you come from!"

The curmudgeon was right about that. Back in Ohio, we never danced in fountains on hot nights, or at any other time for that matter. We never went to bullfights or sang in the street or got thrown out of art classes or had friends hiding from death threats. Our new social life is a *lot* more interesting than the old one.

It sure as hell beats sitting around Cleveland waiting to crumble.

Chapter 8

EAT, DRINK, SMOKE

❧

Whenever we introduced Spanish friends to our dog, Pie, they took one look at her fulsome beauty and commented, "*Tiene buena boca*" (literally "she has a good mouth," meaning a hearty appetite). It was true. The only thing Pie liked better than food was more food. She never begged, she just developed a repertoire of coquettish looks and alluring poses that even the most jaded hearts found difficult to resist. When food was tossed to her, she'd leap joyfully in the air to catch it, gobble it down, and then sit with her head tilted to one side, grinning engagingly at her benefactor. It was a masterful performance by a skilled hustler.

In Ohio, whenever there were landscapers or construction crews in the neighborhood, Pie knew to the minute when each crew scheduled its breaks and would materialize on the site just as the Krispy Kreme and McDonald's bags came out. She would sidle up to the workers looking so winsome and adoring that not only did they share their donuts and burgers with her, they started bringing extra helpings just for the fun of feeding her. Some days she'd have three or four extra meals with various crews before staggering home in time to wolf down her own dinner and get a good night's rest to restore herself for the next eat-a-thon. We did our best to compensate by reducing the portions of dog food, but it was a losing battle. Pie loved to eat, and eat she did, often and with great enthusiasm. She was not a slender reed.

The Spanish have a similar attitude toward dining, managing to fit at least five meals into every day: first breakfast, second breakfast, lunch, afternoon snack, tapas, possibly dinner after that, and on very late nights, hot chocolate and *churros* (fried dough) in the small hours of the morning. And while a few salads and vegetable dishes may appear on the lunch or dinner table, at most meals, especially those taken away from home, meat is the star of the show. Sevillanos went through some very lean years after the Civil War and are still celebrating the fact that they can afford to dine on meat — especially their favorite, pork, and most especially the famous Spanish *jamón* (ham). Made from pigs raised in cork and oak forests and killed in a village festival every winter, served at virtually every occasion from breakfast to a royal wedding, *jamón* is the cornerstone of the local diet. Which made it pretty difficult for me to confess, during my early days in Seville, that I was a vegetarian.

I didn't have anything against meat; I'd eaten it all my life and enjoyed it. But during Rich's corporate years in the Midwest, when we were dining out three and four nights a week with board members and business associates, I simply couldn't face the pressure of making my way through the huge quantities of beef or lamb staring up at me from my plate. My nerve finally broke one night at the home of two heart surgeons, who served me a steak the size of my head, an entire baked potato piled with sour cream, and green beans oozing around in a lake of butter. "Margarine is *so* unhealthy," our hostess confided. I gamely picked up my knife and began sawing away at the beef, but I knew I had met my match. I finished less than a quarter of the meal, despite what my mother taught me about good girls and good guests eating everything on their plate.

After that I gradually let it be known that I'd become a vegetarian. And although this caused my poor hostesses no end of consternation and fuss and entailed my eating countless packaged garden burgers hastily unearthed from the depths of their freezers, it was less stressful (at least on me) in the long run. That is, until I arrived in Seville and found out about the Spanish love affair with ham.

Sevillanos consider ham one of the fundamental ingredients of life, on the short list with air and water. Spanish *jamón* is nothing like the fleshy pink meat Americans put in their sandwiches. It's akin to Italian prosciutto but with a flavor far more robust, its color a richer, more marbled burgundy, its texture both toothier and more tender. When I first walked into a tiny tapas bar and saw two rows of whole pig legs, trotters and all, suspended from the ceiling by ropes, I couldn't fathom how a small place could sell so much meat. On the countertop, a partially carved leg rested in a wood and metal cradle, and I watched the barman produce a dagger-like knife and slice off pieces so thin I could practically see through them. A bowl of ham scraps stood nearby, ready to sprinkle over everything from spinach to eggs to shellfish. I soon learned it is almost impossible to avoid ham if you're eating out in Seville.

This isn't a new phenomenon. Five hundred years ago, when the Spanish Inquisition was bent on purging the country of Jews and Muslims, whose dietary laws prohibited pork, eating ham was one of the ways you publicly demonstrated you were serious when you said you'd converted to Christianity. Today it's one of the ways you publicly demonstrate you're adapting to Spanish life. Explaining that I was a *vegetariana* drew even more stunned disbelief than my attempts to order *té con leche* instead of coffee.

I held out during the years we were vacationing in Seville every spring, watching Rich and everyone we met rave about the exquisite ham, chorizo, skewers of spiced chicken, and other popular local dishes while I was eating my hundredth meal of *bacalao* (salt cod) and *espinacas con garbanzos* (spinach with garbanzo beans). When we began living full-time in Seville, I kept finding myself in situations like the bullfight on the Portuguese border, where refusing to eat meat would have caused great offense to our hosts and embarrassment to our Spanish friends. And what I ate out of social necessity, I found I truly enjoyed; the ham and other meat dishes were delicious and, thankfully, served in small, manageable portions. I began to think of myself as a "flexitarian," meaning mostly but not strictly vegetarian. Sometime during our second year of living in Seville, I crossed the line and began eating ham of my own free will whenever Rich and I went out to breakfast.

Breakfasting in cafés, munching my *tostada con jamón*, I sometimes noticed older men standing at the bar downing glasses of *fino* (a pale, dry sherry) or *anís*, an aniseed liqueur that comes in a delightful sweet style but for some reason is generally preferred in its dry form, which tastes rather like paint thinner. I once asked Yolanda about the practice of starting the day with this kind of eye-opener, and she explained that when men have to get up early and go do a job, they need something like that to *reanimarse*, reanimate themselves.

Some take longer to reanimate themselves than others, and one benefit of the Spanish system is that the purchase of even a single beverage or *tostada* entitles you to stay at your table or corner of the bar for as long as you like — all day, if you choose. I first observed this phenomenon in the bar across from the vacation apartment we used to rent from Luz, where an old man spent every morning lingering over a single glass of *fino*. This man, who for some obscure reason Rich dubbed "Henry," arrived around nine every day, hobbling in on the arm of a male attendant who would park him on the corner barstool and depart. Henry would lean comfortably against the wall enjoying the morning sun streaming through the open doors as the barman placed a glass of *fino* in front of him. Every five or ten minutes, Henry would raise the glass to his lips in very, very slow motion, take a tiny sip, and replace the glass on the bar. Occasionally he would light a cigarette and take long, lazy puffs until it was burned down to the filter, then he'd stub it out carefully in the ashtray and return to his sips of *fino*. Around lunchtime the attendant would come back, help Henry off the barstool, and escort him home.

I thought Henry's daily outing reflected tremendous compassion on the part of the people who cared for him. Whereas an American's family and health care providers would have made strenuous efforts to break him of such unhealthy habits as smoking and drinking, it was pretty clear Henry's caretakers knew that sitting in that bar gave him reason to live. And really, where was the harm? One great thing about advanced old age is that the long-term effects of bad habits have finally become irrelevant. When we first noticed Henry, he seemed so fragile we were keeping our fingers crossed that he'd last until the end of the month. More than a decade later, he's still contentedly sipping his *fino* on that same corner barstool every morning.

Sevillano breakfasts tend to be simple and solitary, but lunch is a more elaborate and communal affair. The Sevillano lunch is no mere sandwich, no quick carton of yogurt gulped down at the desk surrounded by ringing phones. This is the main meal of the day, and most shops and businesses close from two until five in order to allow people time to collect the kids from school and head home to a family meal or to repair to a nearby café with friends or coworkers.

Many cafés offer a low-cost, three-course *menú del día* (special of the day), which usually includes a choice of two dishes such as *carrillada* (roast pork cheeks), *solomillo al whiskey* (grilled pork loin in a whiskey sauce with whole cloves of garlic), *cola de toro* (stewed bull's tail), *pollo a la mostaza* (chicken with mustard sauce), *lomo con salsa dulce* (grilled pork with a sweet sauce of wine and raisins), *lentejas con chorizo* (lentil soup with chunks of chorizo sausage), or *tortilla española* (a dense omelet with onions and potatoes). The *menú del día* usually includes a *cerveza* (beer) served ice-cold in an eight-ounce glass, making the portion small enough be drunk down before it has time to warm up. The third course is a dessert, such as ice cream, an orange, or a "*huevo frito*" (literally "fried egg"), which turns out to be a golden half peach surrounded by a pool of whipped cream.

Construction workers, street cleaners, the *costaleros* who carry religious platforms in the processions, and others who do hard physical labor are considered entitled to enjoy *cerveza* with their *menú del día* at midday. They can often be seen downing a liter of beer during the morning break and again at lunch; they rarely appear to be drunk, but they clearly aren't entirely sober either.

The prevalence of beer at the luncheon table of laborers may — I'm just guessing here — account for the high accident rates on so many Sevillano work sites. A few years ago an American I knew was hired to improve the safety of Europe's largest copper mine, which is located near Seville. When he suggested that the miners stop going to bars and drinking a liter of beer with their midday meal, everyone looked at him blankly, as if to say, "I understand the words but don't really take your meaning. Why don't we go have a beer and talk it over?" He eventually prevailed, and today the miners have an alcohol-free catered lunch; safety records have soared, although morale has not.

For those of us who aren't doing heavy physical labor, the *menú del día* may be a bit too generous. I usually prefer to order a tapa or two, or if I'm with friends, share a *ración* (full plate) or *media ración* (half plate) of whatever is going around, such as pork loin or fried fish, washing the food down with a small frosty beer. After that, I am more than ready to enjoy my siesta. When I get up, my *merienda* (afternoon snack) is enough to tide me over until dinner at nine thirty or ten. While normally my dinner is nothing more than a tapa or two in a café or a hearty bowl of soup at home, when I'm invited to a Sevillano friend's for dinner, I know it will be a considerably more elaborate affair.

The normal start time for a dinner party is nine thirty, and by now Rich and I have learned to come bearing a frothy dessert or box of chocolates as a hostess gift. After meeting everyone and exchanging greetings and kisses (or in Rich's case, manly handshakes with the *hombres*), we all sit down around a coffee table, at which point our host offers us all small glasses of cold beer.

I know what you're thinking: what's all this endless talk about beer, when everyone's raving about Spanish wine these days? The Sevillanos love their wine too, but due to the extremely hot summers in Andalucía, most have fallen into the habit of refreshing themselves with ice-cold beer or occasionally — and I don't mean to horrify the purists — red wine poured over ice and mixed with a fizzy beverage similar to 7Up, a concoction known as *tinto de verano* (red wine of summer).

When I first arrived in Seville and expressed a preference for my customary glass of white wine before dinner, people stared at me, and inevitably somebody would make a jocular comment about how I was heading fast toward inebriation. I thought they were insane, of course, until I noticed their words held a kernel of truth. Maybe it's because everyone is chronically dehydrated by the climate, and beer's higher liquid-to-alcohol ratio works to our advantage, but I soon found that a beer eased me into a long night of revelry far more gracefully than wine.

After that first beer goes down the parched throat, many people do switch to wine, usually a rich *vino tinto* (red wine) from northern Spain's Rioja or Ribera del Duero regions. One of the things I love about Sevillanos is that they consider wine a part of the food experience, not a fetish or a drug. While appreciating the taste and effects of a good glass of *vino*, Sevillanos will not summon the sommelier for a twenty-minute discussion of the 2004 vintage versus the 2006, nor will they spend half an hour praising the wine's complexities and arguing about whether it has an undertone of raspberry, smoke, or autumn leaves. Commentary is usually limited to "Hey, this is great. Let me pour you another glass." Nor do most people drink to get soused; like their food, their alcohol tends to be consumed in moderate amounts at frequent intervals.

At Spanish dinner parties, the intervals can get a little too frequent for my comfort, since my capacity for drink is famously low. It's not so much that I'm likely to make a fool of myself (who needs alcohol for that?), but I get horribly sleepy. And my mom taught me that when I'm a dinner guest in someone's home, I am supposed to remain conscious the entire time, if at all possible.

When we all have beer in hand, the hostess will begin producing small plates of olives, slivers of ham, triangles of cheese, and mounds of *picos,* the short, hard breadsticks that are a mainstay in the nibbling cuisine of Seville. Along with the second round of beer and the first appearance of wine, the hostess will produce a stack of small plates and a clutch of forks. While these are being shared out, she'll go back into the kitchen again and again, bringing out platters of cold roast pork, wafer-thin rounds of chorizo, wedges of *tortilla,* an *ensaladilla* (literally "little salad," referring to any mayonnaise-laden cold mixture, often with potatoes and shrimp), *empanada de atún* (a thin pie filled with tuna and vegetables), and *medianoches* ("midnights," small sandwiches made of soft rolls, cheese, and pink, British-style ham).

At this point in the first such dinner party I attended, I was already full and nearly panicking, thinking that we were still in the appetizer phase of the evening and would soon be ushered to a dining table to begin the heavy-duty eating of the night. But it turned out that the entire meal would be served at the coffee table, in the comfort of sofas and armchairs. Although meals are often served at conventional dining room tables as well, I love the casual atmosphere of the coffee-table meal and often entertain my guests this way.

At a typical dinner party, most of the food served to this point has been cold and was probably purchased at a local market, delicatessen, or restaurant; cooking has not caught on as a fad in Seville. But for the grand finale, the hostess will usually carry in her own culinary contribution, such as a thick, brown pork stew with potatoes and peas.

Even nibbling the minimal mounts required of a good guest, I am always more than replete at this stage, but of course, there is more to come.

The cheerful pop of a cork heralds the arrival of *cava*, the local version of champagne, which has more flavor and fewer bubbles than its French cousin. Then the desserts float in, great frothy concoctions with six layers of cake separated by whipped cream and topped with frosting in cunning swirls and peaks. Unfortunately, these gorgeous creations are more a feast for the eye than the palate, being sugary and bland, without even a touch of vanilla to provide flavor.

By now it's around midnight, and I am glassy-eyed with food, drink, and the effort of following a Spanish conversation that's bouncing around among half a dozen people whose alcohol levels are inspiring them to speak with even greater speed and less clarity than usual. Luckily, trays of chocolates are likely to appear next, and I'll pop one or two in my mouth, letting the sugar rush revive my drooping eyelids. Now the host brings out bottles of gin, whiskey, rum, tonic, and Coca-Cola and begins offering everyone mixed drinks. I gratefully switch to tonic water, as do many of the other women. Half an hour later, while we're all picking at the remains of the cakes and chocolates, the liqueurs come out, including Miura, a local favorite made by nuns from wild cherries and aniseed, which is like drinking cough syrup over ice.

Somewhere around two in the morning, the guests start taking their leave, and Rich and I stagger out into the night. Most of our friends live thirty or forty minutes' walk from our apartment, and a stroll through the cool night air helps us clear our heads and work off at least a little of the food and drink we've just consumed.

So why, with all this eating and drinking, aren't the Sevillanos even fatter than our dog, Pie? More to the point, why wasn't I gaining weight? Here I had abandoned my long-held, low-fat vegetarian diet, committing a host of sins with *jamón,* fried fish, chocolate, and beer. Yet my weight actually went down a little, and I knew I looked and felt fitter. How was this possible? And what next? Was I about to learn that recycling actually harms the planet, driving sober increases the chances of car accidents, and cigarettes prevent cancer? Just how upside-down was my worldview going to get?

So far, no one has tried to convince me of any of those things. But during my first year in Seville, as I violated one fundamental nutritional belief after another with apparent impunity, I began to develop some theories (or possibly rationalizations) to explain the phenomenon.

First of all, while my diet is extremely rich, the amount I eat (when not at dinner parties) is quite small. I consume less but never feel hungry, because in place of mountains of low-fat food, I'm eating small portions of dishes that are truly satisfying to palate and stomach.

The other reason I feel so healthy is that I walk everywhere. In a city like Seville, traveling by foot is simply the most practical way to get around. The convoluted street plan, with its overabundance of one-ways and dead-ends — to say nothing of the narrow streets crowded with illegally parked vehicles — makes driving in the city center a nightmare. Living in the Ohio countryside, I averaged two hours in the car every day; now I spend that amount of time strolling through the city to visit the shops, markets, cafés, gymnasium, friends' homes, museums, theaters, and other places that make up the daily round. On the rare occasion when Rich and I want to go out of the city, we rent a car or travel with friends. Many Spanish and expat friends have cars, especially if they have kids or need to travel for business; but even then, if they live in the city, walking is their first choice.

Among all the other advantages, the pedestrian lifestyle means no one has to serve as the designated driver and spend the night drinking *cerveza sin alcohol* (alcohol-free beer), known as *sin* for short.

Entertaining in the expat community is somewhat less elaborate than the typical Spanish dinner party and, in my early days of living in Seville, usually involved activities organized by the women's club. Along with the welcome committee tapas nights, I introduced another type of fiesta: wine tastings.

As a fourth-generation Californian who grew up just south of Napa Valley's famous vineyards, I was surprised to discover that the Spanish didn't make more of a fuss about their wines. Well into my first year living in Seville, I was a trifle embarrassed to realize I couldn't comment at all, much less intelligently, on the rival merits of the local vintages. In an attempt to correct this deficiency, I decided to organize a wine tasting for the women's club.

The invitations went out, and twenty people signed up, including women from half a dozen countries, many of whom brought along Spanish husbands or boyfriends. Into this international group, I brought in a Spanish presenter who spoke enough English to provide us with elaborate commentary on the origins and characteristics of each vintage. Everyone listened politely until he stopped talking, then immediately broke into animated conversations with their neighbors about movies, books, politics, tattoos, fall fashions... anything but the wine. I soon learned that what people really wanted to do was sample a few wines without ever having to pause in the headlong rush that characterizes the local conversational style. So we stopped having presenters and just put the bottles of wine on the table with their labels hidden and challenged people to match the flavor of the wine with some printed descriptions taken off the Internet. Everyone had a marvelous time. If we didn't learn a lot about the wines, at least we were fully up to date about one another's tastes and opinions about movies, books, politics, tattoos, and fall fashions.

There was one alcoholic beverage that our European friends expressed a keen interest in learning more about: the martini. They had watched everyone from James Bond to Don Draper sipping them in Hollywood productions, and they knew they were the essence of cool, but few had ever tried one. What were they like, exactly?

Rich, who loves martinis, explained they could not be described, only experienced, and offered to arrange it. We then made several attempts to order martinis in the city's better bars, with exceedingly disappointing results. Once we made an advance visit to a fancy hotel bar to explain in great detail what we wanted. The bartender looked down his nose at us and replied rather stiffly that he was accustomed to serving *el martini* and would be happy to do so on any occasion on which we felt inclined to patronize his establishment. We returned the next day with friends, and Rich ordered a round of martinis, specifying his usual three olives. A short while later a waiter strode in, majestically bearing aloft a tray holding the classic triangular glasses, which seemed promising, although the color of the liquid, a pale green, did not. It took but a single sip to determine that they'd served us unadulterated Martini & Rossi sweet vermouth, with three rather bewildered-looking olives floating in each glass.

After several such bitter disillusionments, we decided there was only one solution: we would throw a martini party for Rich's upcoming birthday. Knowing that many of the guests were unacquainted with the pleasures and pitfalls of martini consumption, I sent out an invitation explaining that these were delightful but extremely powerful beverages that should be treated with respect. By way of illustration I quoted a poem I'd heard attributed to Dorothy Parker:

I like to have a martini,
Two at the very most.
After three I'm under the table,
After four I'm under my host.

"If I drink four, do I get to be under the host*ess*?" asked our friend Héctor, who seemed to regard the poem as a challenge rather than a warning.

"We'll talk after your third," I said, feeling fairly certain he'd never get past number two.

But Héctor was thirty, in the full flower of his young manhood; half Spanish, half American, and filled with bravado, he felt confident he was strong enough to stand up to any drink that an older fellow like Rich could handle. Héctor downed his first martini in fifteen minutes, the second in just over half an hour. "Better slow down there, buddy," Rich kindly advised, but by now Héctor was in no condition to listen. He guzzled the third and took one swallow of his fourth.

And then he vanished into my bathroom and didn't come out for the next three and a half hours.

His wife went in to tend to him, and then another friend who, as a masseuse, was held to have something akin to a medical background. As you can imagine, everyone had a great deal of good-natured fun at Héctor's expense, but the jokes were tinged with sympathy, because there were few at the party who hadn't done something equally idiotic in their day.

One of the enormous advantages of getting older is that you can look back almost fondly on the embarrassing excesses of your youth, resting in the happy knowledge that you haven't committed that particular kind of folly in decades. And poor Héctor did us one good turn: his prolonged and (we could only imagine) horrific sufferings served as a far more potent warning than Dorothy Parker's poem. The rest of our guests sipped their martinis warily, and most soon shifted back to the safer pleasures of wine or beer. No one became so snookered as to require the use of our second bathroom for more than a brief visit. By the time a shamefaced Héctor emerged around two in the morning and slipped out the front door, our friends were glowing with the satisfaction of having mastered the exotic art of drinking martinis — and of avoiding Héctor's fate.

Alcohol is such an accepted fact of Spanish life that the government makes little effort to control the drinking habits of the population, but it has undertaken the equally thankless task of trying to rein in the nation's tobacco consumption. When I arrived in Seville, it seemed as if everyone smoked, including my doctor and the young woman who worked at the health food store. Many considered it one of the basic pleasures of life and a health risk worth taking, in much the same way Americans consume considerably more sugar than they know is good for them. A famous Spanish ad campaign positioned smoking as a matter of personal freedom; its slogan, "I choose," ran beneath photos such as a naked man capering joyfully in a field or two pretty girls kissing passionately. Upon seeing the ad with the girls, an American visitor turned to me in surprise, saying, "The lesbians here advertise? That's how they recruit?" I hastened to explain that the ad was promoting smoking, not switching to the other team.

Arriving from an ever more smoke-free America, I found it tough at first to adjust to the choking atmosphere in cafés and bars; after an evening out, I'd wake up coughing and wondering uneasily just how much damage my lungs were sustaining from the secondhand smoke. A lesser but more immediate concern was the way my entire wardrobe began to smell unpleasantly of secondhand tobacco. Just walking from an outdoor table through the café to the restroom was enough to saturate a sweater with sufficient fumes to permeate my entire closet. It was simply impractical to send sweaters and jackets to the dry cleaners after every outing, so when I got home I'd hang them in the hallway or window to air them out. If only I could do that with my lungs, I thought.

Eventually, after years of spirited wrangling, Spain managed to pass a highly controversial law banning smoking in all bars and restaurants that measured more than one thousand square meters. Since nearly all Seville's bars fall far short of that size, their owners rushed to post signs on their doors that read SE FUMA AQUÍ (one smokes here). I was relieved to discover that the signs meant smoking was *allowed* but not actually *required* in those establishments, many of which were favorite hangouts of mine. Nearly all Seville's interesting nightlife took place in little backstreet places where the air was thick with smoke, animated conversation, the cheerful clink of glasses, and at times, the wailing voices and stomping feet of flamenco artists. Everyone continued puffing away in these bars with unabated pleasure.

Luckily for my lungs and my wardrobe, the Spanish government eventually passed a new law that banned smoking in all public bars and restaurants. This news, celebrated by so many in the expat community, was greeted with dismay by L-F and Simone. They smoke sparingly, and never in front of their children, but find it difficult to hold a late-night philosophical discussion without a generous supply of what they refer to, in the British manner, as "fags." As a result, the four of us usually dine at outdoor tables well into the chillier parts of winter and far too early in the spring. We sit outside for hours, bundled in coats and scarves, drinking beer or wine, arguing about such topics as why people fear death, how technology is affecting children's learning patterns, and whether or not this light drizzle really warrants heading inside the café.

One thing I know for certain: I am willing to risk a chill, even secondhand smoke, for true *amigos.* Sitting with good friends, nibbling ham and olives, sipping drinks, and trying to express how we truly think and feel about what's most important to us — life just doesn't get better than that.

As the Spanish saying goes, *el vino, para que sepa a vino, bébelo con un amigo* — for wine to taste like wine, you must drink it with a friend.

Chapter 9

MOVES

One afternoon about two years after we'd moved to Seville, I was walking down a street near our apartment when I heard a loud wolf whistle. Glancing around, noticing that I was the only woman on the street, I kind of perked up, thinking, "Hey, I've still got it!" Then the whistle came again, and again — until I finally realized it was a parrot.

I described this lowering moment to Yolanda, who was then in her early forties. She told me she had recently passed by a construction site, and all the men were whistling and giving the local equivalent of "hubba hubba" until the foreman shouted, "Have some respect, boys, she's old enough to be your mother." She told me, "That kind of respect I *don't* need!"

As she was telling me this, we were picking our way down a narrow street past some workmen clearing rubble. One of the men called out to the others, "Get these rocks out of the way. We don't want these flowers" — he bowed in our direction — "to fall." That kind of old-fashioned gallantry, known as a *piropo*, was common in Spain before wolf whistles and "hubba hubba" came into fashion. It was comforting to know that some of the old ways lingered on, even in these changing times.

And times were definitely changing that year. I don't know what it was — Mercury in retrograde? A disturbance in the Force? The thinning of the ozone layer? — but the winds of change were blowing through my life at gale-force speed. They brought the good, the bad, and the ugly, and everything in between. I'm not even going to get into the sad little losses, such as more new friends moving away, or the infuriating ones, like having my purse snatched by a passing motorcyclist practically in front of my apartment. No, I am talking about major shocks and upheavals now.

I'll get the worst one over right away: our beloved dog, Pie, passed away that spring, after thirteen years by my side. She had lately grown creaky and cranky, eccentric in behavior, and clearly uncomfortable much of the time. Her walks grew shorter, and even visits with Bruno in the park seemed to lose their luster. More shockingly, food failed to hold her interest anymore. Finally the vet did some tests and showed us that the compassionate choice was to end her suffering. She suggested gently that we take Pie home for a week, give her every comfort, then bring her back. It was one of the saddest weeks I've ever known. When the time came, Molly and Mauri drove us to the vet, since Pie could no longer manage the short walk on her own. There, Rich and I held Pie's warm, furry body for the last time, letting her know she was loved as she let out her final breath.

We were heartbroken. I remember walking through the city in a haze of grief for days. Rich collected Pie's ashes, and we went together to scatter some in the park where she'd played with Bruno and some behind the beer barrels in her favorite bar; from what I've seen of their cleaning standards, her ashes will be a permanent fixture. The rest of her ashes were set aside to be brought back to Ohio and placed in our garden, under the shrub where she liked to snooze away hot afternoons. Pie's timing, as always, was impeccable; that summer would mark our last chance to do anything at that house, because Rich and I had finally made the decision to sell it.

Just two years earlier, such a decision would have been unthinkable. We had moved into that house as newlyweds, built a wonderful life there, and planned to leave it feetfirst in a pine box. We had lavished love and labor on the house and garden, built friendships in the neighborhood, and considered our home a fundamental part of who we were as individuals and as a couple. To walk away from it would mean walking away from a thousand cherished memories that made up our shared past.

But the time had come to decide whether our future lay in Cleveland or in Seville. Rich and I had settled into a new life we found fuller, richer, and more satisfying, a life that forced us to grow rather than making it all too easy to stagnate. The longer we lived in Seville, the less inclined we were to return to our old life. Sitting in sunny sidewalk cafés all that spring, while Ohio hunkered down in the grip of snowstorms and bone-chilling cold, Rich and I spent hours discussing our options. We finally concluded that we weren't going back to live in the US at any time in the foreseeable future. And if we were not going to live there, did it still make sense to spend the time, money, and mental effort it took to maintain an old country house and acres of property from thousands of miles away?

Since moving to Seville, we had gone back to Ohio only once, for the six-week visit the previous summer to make the necessary arrangements to extend our stay in Spain for a second year. While we were in Cleveland, I had found it difficult to motivate myself to spend countless hours repainting trim and weeding flower beds that I didn't expect to see again for a year. That part didn't faze Rich, who loves home improvement and gardening projects unreservedly, but back in Seville he used to lie awake nights worrying about burst pipes and squirrels nibbling away on our power lines (this had happened before and did not end well for either the power lines or the squirrel). He pictured our pine trees catching on fire again, as they'd done twice due to electrical lines rubbing against the trunks, and he imagined tall oaks uprooting and falling over onto the house, as had happened to our next-door neighbors. He spent a lot of time exchanging emails with maintenance people, making sure the trees were trimmed of dead branches, the leaves were raked, the gutters cleaned, and mousetraps checked on a timely basis. Watching him fret about the house made me all the more certain we had to let go of it.

Although I knew all this in my heart of hearts, it took me a very, very long time to be able to say aloud, "We should sell the house." At first it felt like voicing the suggestion that I should amputate a part of my own body. It was worse than giving up my security blanket when I was four. But just like my beloved blanket, what was right for one phase of my life was now holding me back from the next. In a matter of weeks, the idea of selling went from unimaginable to a possibility to a probability to a certainty.

So now we were ready to sell, but would anyone be ready to buy? The real estate market had started going into serious freefall in the run-up to the global economic recession. Where desirable homes in our part of Ohio had once been snapped up in a matter of weeks, it was now taking a year or two and lots of price reductions to close a deal. We figured we would get it on the market in May and hope for a nibble by fall. We contacted a real estate agent who lived in our neighborhood and sat back to wait.

Four days after the house was listed, we had three firm offers at our full asking price. We went with the first offer, and over the next ten days our real estate agent negotiated the timing, inspections, financing, and all the other details with the prospective owners. One of the few real stumbling blocks was the schedule: the new owners were determined to be in by the end of July. Obviously this would be a tremendous inconvenience to us, but I wanted to do the deal and move on with our lives.

"But we're not going back to the States until mid-June," Rich objected sensibly. "Can we really clear out twenty years' worth of stuff in just five weeks?"

"Don't be silly. It's not five weeks, it's more like three and a half; don't forget, we have to drive to New Jersey for your brother's seventieth birthday party and fly back to California for my family's annual reunion."

Rich paled a little. "Can we do it in three and a half weeks?"

"Of course. I have a plan."

Scanned documents flew back and forth until at last the deal was nearly done. Late one night, the final sale agreement was signed and scanned and ready to go; all we had to do was hit "send" and the house would belong to the new owners. I noticed my hands were shaking. I was sure we were doing the right thing, really I was, but now that the decision was on the brink of becoming irrevocable, I felt a momentary stab of anxiety that was close to panic.

"Last chance to back out," said Rich. "You're still sure?"

I took a deep breath. "Absolutely. But wait one minute." I ran to the kitchen and poured two small shots of Rich's favorite Cuban rum over ice. I handed one to him, and we clinked glasses and each took a long swallow. "Okay," I said. "Let's do it." I moved the curser to hover over the email's Send button; we both put our fingers on the computer's trackpad and pressed down. The email was sent. The house was no longer ours.

Neither of us has ever regretted the decision. The timing, however, did complicate our lives considerably.

In June we flew back to Ohio and hit the ground running. I became ruthlessly organized, making a chart of the house and a plan for clearing out one room every day. Triage consisted of separating things into piles to pack, to set aside for the garage sale, and to toss in the trash. My sister Kate, who has moved a lot in her life, passed along one invaluable rule: if anyone in the family wants to keep an item, you keep it. No discussion. That saved hours, maybe days, of time right there. I borrowed some long tables from a neighbor and set them up the garage, so all garage sale items could be put directly in place. All items to be packed for storage were stacked in the middle of the cleared room. Extra trash pickup was arranged. It was all systems go.

We were up at six every morning, attacking the room of the day. We started with the attic over the garage where Rich had his office, and we soon agreed that many boxes of old records could and should be destroyed. At the time we didn't know of a shredding service, so we used our own home shredder, which soon broke down; we bought a second, which also collapsed under the strain. Finally we gave up and started burning the stuff in the fireplace, waiting until nightfall when the temperature would go down to eighty degrees. "So this is hell," Rich remarked as we wiped the dripping sweat off our faces and tossed more folders onto the blaze.

In spare time that we didn't have, Rich and I made dozens of minor repairs to the house and grounds to comply with the terms of the sale agreement; visited our financial advisors, doctors, and dentists; and went out to dinners, lunches, and coffee with old friends. I normally don't drink coffee, since it makes me too nervous to sleep, but I was starting every day with a Starbucks run and dozing off in front of the fire every night; it's a wonder I didn't fall in and burn to death.

At one of the doctor's visits, I received unwelcome news: I needed another surgery on my right wrist. Some years earlier I'd had some noncancerous cysts removed, which the doctor had blithely assured was a minor surgery from which I'd completely recover in six weeks or so. In fact, it was a year before I could pick up a stack of dinner plates or practice yoga, and the scar zigzagging down my wrist still looks like the result of an attack by Lord Voldemort.

So you can imagine my vexation upon learning, three years later in the midst of a whirlwind move, that I would need a second, similar operation. I decided the surgery would have to wait; I had plans for that wrist during the weeks ahead. There was no way I was clearing out my house and running a garage sale without it.

Our neighbor Nancy, who was an expert in garage sales, came over to cast an appraising eye over the things we were getting ready to sell.

"Three days," she said. "Thursday, Friday, and Saturday."

"Not Sunday?"

"Never on Sunday; you just get lookers, nobody buys on Sundays."

Who knew? Our sale items soon overflowed the garage and filled the barn, the shed, and the screened porch as well. We put a notice in the paper and on Craigslist, and Nancy went out the morning of the sale to hang balloons and signs on the street corners. Some of the big items, such as the generator and the tractor, were sold ahead of time through newspaper ads, but the vast majority of the stuff was spread out for the world to pick over.

The garage sale was actually good fun. It was like a three-day neighborhood party where instead of a hostess gift, everyone brought us money and took away things we no longer wanted. The sheer volume of possessions we'd collected over the years had begun to feel overwhelming, a heavy burden we'd been carrying without even realizing it. Every item that departed was a small but heartfelt relief. We didn't really care when people pilfered things — mostly pocketknives that Rich had somehow accumulated over the years, which were set out in the one corner of the garage that was hard to surveil from the cash table on the driveway.

Almost without exception, our customers wandered onto the back deck and exclaimed, "My *God*, look at this *view*! How can you *stand* to leave it?" I felt a pang of regret every time someone said it, and Nancy, being a true friend, soon took care of this. The moment someone uttered the words, "My *God*—" she would ruthlessly interrupt and say, "But let me show you what's on the back porch," and drag them off to spend more money.

By Saturday afternoon we had sold an amazing amount of stuff, made thousands of dollars, and were more or less giving things away. On Sunday we invited back one of our Saturday customers, a Ukrainian woman with a large family and slender means, and told her to take any leftovers she wanted. Later that afternoon a friend's father arrived to collect the remains for charity. As his enormous boat of a Buick sailed away up the driveway, stuffed with the very last of the garage sale items, we were done.

On Monday professional movers arrived to pack up everything we were keeping. Rich and I spent the next three days following them around, relabeling the boxes. Left to their own devices, the crew had a tendency to write on every box "Contents: knick knacks," or as some of them liked to spell it, "nik nax." At the end of the third day, they loaded up everything on a truck and hauled it off to a storage unit until that far distant time when we would own real estate in the US again.

We spent the night at Nancy's, and the next day three Amish women — grandmother, mother, and daughter — arrived to give the house a final cleaning. They were incredible, especially the grandmother, who came up to my shoulder and leapt nimbly up and down stepladders wielding dust rags and soap buckets with wiry strength. By late afternoon they were gone, the house shining, clean, and empty. Rich was off picking up some records at his doctor's office, and I was alone in the house for a while, saying a private and tearful farewell. I didn't for a moment regret our decision, but it was still painful to part with something I had loved so much. When Rich arrived to collect me, he took one look at my face, dragged me off to Nancy's, and poured wine down my throat until I regained my composure.

We flew out the next day, but not to Spain. The end of July is no time to be in Seville, where triple-digit temperatures are the norm and spikes of 125 or more are all too common. Instead, Rich and I had made arrangements to spend the rest of the summer in California, renting a small apartment in San Francisco while we visited relatives and friends we hadn't seen in a while.

I love San Francisco — or the City, as it's known locally; no one who's from there would be caught dead referring to it as San Fran or Frisco. Rich and I had been toying with the idea that someday, in the far distant future, we might buy a little place in the City to be our pied-à-terre during our US visits. That notion died within hours of stepping off the plane. How could we have forgotten the truth of the saying, so famously and mistakenly attributed to Mark Twain, "Coldest winter I ever spent was one summer in San Francisco"? In late July, arriving in sandals and shorts from the sweltering heat of Ohio, we found temperatures in the mid-fifties with gray skies and a bitter wind that was blowing the trees sideways. And it didn't let up for weeks. There is a scientific explanation involving ocean, bay, hills, valleys, inversion layers, the Japanese current, and probably chaos theory, but none of that made it any easier to spend August shivering in a winter parka. It was especially galling because twenty minutes away in every direction, people were blissfully basking half-naked in the sun, sipping iced drinks and languidly trying to decide if it was too hot to barbeque something for dinner. In less time than it takes to tell, San Francisco was off our short list.

But we were too busy to give much serious thought to California real estate. Because it turned out that not only did I have to find a doctor and arrange for my wrist surgery, but Rich had his own, more serious health concern. While I had been saying my tearful farewells to the house, Rich was picking up medical records at his dermatologist's office. The nurse had casually mentioned over the phone that they'd found something he ought to take care of, but he wasn't seriously concerned. He has the kind of skin that often produces small pre-precancerous growths that are burned off in the doctor's office, and he assumed that was the case now. They handed him a file without a word, and he opened it up to read: Melanoma. Skin cancer.

There was no time to consult anyone in Ohio before we left, and Rich waited until we'd been in California for three days, and I had recuperated a little from the stress of the move, before he told me about it. It was the worst moment in a year that had seen quite a few bad moments. I was shocked speechless.

But not for long. As soon as I got my voice back, I called a doctor friend in Ohio and read him the dermatologist's report; he reassured us that it sounded as if the problem area was on the surface, making it far from life-threatening. Most likely it could be completely removed via a relatively simple surgical procedure. If possible, our friend recommended, Rich should have something called Mohs surgery, which was less invasive and would result in less scarring. As it turned out, San Francisco had one of the few surgeons in America who performed Mohs surgery in cases like this, and Rich got on his schedule for early September.

Anxieties about my wrist operation were utterly overshadowed by this new worry, and I sailed through the surgery — which, as it turned out, was far less debilitating than the first one. By the time Rich's Mohs surgery rolled around, I was still sporting an arm brace but was well on the road to recovery.

We arrived at the appointed time for Rich's surgery, and for reasons that I will never comprehend, the surgeon insisted I stay in the room throughout the procedure. I can only suppose he wanted someone to chat with during the long, dull stretches when he was fiddling around with the cell layers. "So, I understand you two live in Seville part of the year," he remarked in a conversational tone, and I started telling him, rather distractedly, about our lives there, trying to ignore what else was going on in the room. From descriptions on the Mohs surgery website, I had built up an image of the kind of bloodless incision you see in science fiction movies, where they pass a wand over the area and the job's done. Not so! The procedure turned out to be less like *Star Trek* and more like a scene from *The Terminator.* I shuddered to think what non-Mohs surgery would have looked like.

When it was all over, the original, grape-sized area of concern had been replaced by a rakish scar that ran from the corner of Rich's mouth to the bottom of his chin. "Too bad it's not Halloween," I told him. "A couple of bolts and your Frankenstein costume would be complete."

The doctor sent us home with instructions for Rich to take all his meals through a straw and to come back the following week to get the stitches out. The final checkup would be in three weeks, just before we returned to Seville. The doctor wasn't happy about Rich flying off even then, but we'd already delayed our return to Spain by ten days, and for reasons I probably don't need to spell out for you, we were ready to put this summer behind us.

In the days that followed his procedure, Rich's spirits were understandably a bit low. So to cheer him up, I suggested that we go out and look at some real estate. Not that we were interested in any immediate way, but it would help us get a feel for the market and weigh the rival merits of various parts of the Bay Area in preparation for the far-distant day when we might buy a place there.

This perked Rich up considerably, and he spent many happy hours on the Internet doing research and talking (as best he could, with only three-quarters of his face mobile) to real estate agents all over the Bay Area. Having eliminated the City itself, on the basis of the horrible summer weather, we began exploring various other options. With relatives in the East Bay, south of the City in Silicon Valley, and north of the Golden Gate Bridge in Marin County, we received plenty of conflicting advice about where we should start looking.

When we did look at homes, we tried not to gasp out loud at the prices. For what we'd received for our beautiful old stone house on nearly four acres of land with ancient oak trees and a spectacular view of a wooded valley, we could just about afford a small cottage or a sterile new condo with a view of the freeway. Didn't these people know that real estate values were plummeting? The agents assured us these prices *were* reduced, and we were lucky to be looking now.

Our search eventually narrowed to Marin County, the area just north of San Francisco across the Golden Gate Bridge. We had always known that Marin was a weird mix of upscale and scruffy; it appealed to people for whom lifestyle mattered, whether that meant opening a hundred-dollar bottle of Chardonnay every night or smoking medical marijuana on the back deck. Movie greats such as George Lucas and Sean Penn lived there, as did dot-com millionaires and business executives from the City, along with artists, writers, musicians, burned-out hippies, and people who were convinced they were Jesus Christ, kept wolves as pets, or practiced witchcraft when the moon was full. Whenever I saw a guy walking around in his pajamas talking to himself, I was never sure whether he'd gone off his meds again or was making a multimillion-dollar deal on a phone so tiny it was invisible.

One of the attractions of Marin was the vast network of parks and hiking trails adjacent to a string of small towns that were walking distance apart. Having grown used to going everywhere on foot in Seville, we were reluctant to recommit to the American car culture, which makes driving the only practical mode of transportation in 99 percent of the country.

A few days after Rich's surgery, we took a temporary apartment in Marin County. We'd been staying in San Francisco, first at one short-term rental apartment and then, when we extended our stay for the surgery, at a second that was available only part of the time we needed. Our third California home that summer was a small in-law cottage in a pretty little town called Larkspur.

After unpacking our few belongings and many medical supplies, we walked down the street to the local saloon for a beer. The bartender took one look at Rich's bandaged face and the brace on my wrist and said, "What did you do, lady, slug him one?" I said, "Yes, he pissed me off. And if I were you, I'd watch my step." He slid the beers over to us and backed away without another word. I loved it. Normally it's next to impossible for me to pull off being intimidating. Looking as if I had come out on top in a brawl was a new sensation for me. When strangers asked about my arm brace, I took to saying, "You should see the other guy."

Rich began spending most of his waking hours thinking about real estate, aided and abetted by a fellow addict, my sister Kate. She had lived in various parts of Marin over the past twenty years and knew the turf the way Rich knew Chagrin Falls, Ohio. The two of them conferred daily, discussing the newest listings and comparing features and prices.

One morning Kate called to tell us about a cottage that had just come on the market in San Anselmo, the next town over from where she was living at the time. The new listing was a two-story, brown-shingled cottage tucked away in a quiet lane behind the police station and public library, just blocks from the sleepy little downtown area. And the price — only 20 percent more than we'd received for our home in Ohio — was what passed for affordable in Marin County. We agreed to go take a look.

I loved the cottage at first sight. Built in 1900, it had grown quirky over the years with built-ins and add-ons. Except for a few midcentury modern missteps, such as aluminum windows and chipped Formica counters, the house had preserved its original charm. The front was sheltered from view by a fence covered with a tangle of vines, and the back had a weathered wooden fence, a tiny garden with a wooden deck, and towering bamboo that went a long way to obscure the fact that there was a two-story apartment building next door.

"We're just looking, right?" I said, seeing the gleam in Rich's eye. "We're not actually ready to buy yet, are we?"

But apparently we were.

Rich began laying out his reasons. I had not until that moment realized how deeply the health scare had affected his outlook on life. Not surprisingly, he felt unusually vulnerable, and it didn't help that we had just cut our ties with the home that had sheltered us for twenty years. Rich is a profound optimist, but he always comes up with a plan to deal with the worst-case scenario, and now he wanted to establish a base in his home country, a base that came surrounded by a support group of family, longtime friends, and doctors capable of performing Mohs surgery. Finding a house we both loved in a great location, Rich suddenly saw his way clear to establishing a safe haven in a world that was feeling all too uncertain at the moment. It didn't mean we were turning our backs on the adventure of living in Seville, it just meant we had a fallback position, a place to go should there ever be another unwelcome diagnosis. It was the only form of protection he could mount against a future we both desperately hoped to avoid.

I was a little shocked at myself for not having realized sooner just how deep his concerns ran or how much he needed someplace to call "home" in America. If buying the house would help, I was all for it. I fervently prayed we would never have to live there out of medical necessity. But even if we did not, buying the place had a lot to recommend it: providing us with a comfortable place to stay while visiting relatives and friends in the Bay Area, avoiding any more summers spent bouncing around from one rental unit to another. And most of all, giving Rich some peace of mind.

In short, we bought the house.

The next weeks were a blur of paperwork and inspections and calls to the storage unit in Ohio to arrange for the transfer of our possessions. Rich was in his glory with a real estate deal in the works; it made a welcome distraction from the Frankenstein scar, bandage changes, and follow-up doctor visits. The young couple currently living in our future home wouldn't be out until October, so we flew back to Seville and finished up the final paperwork over the Internet. We became official owners in October but wouldn't take possession until we returned to California in January.

It was at this point that we established a new pattern in our lives: we would spend eight months of the year in Seville and return to San Anselmo for three months in the summer and for five weeks every winter. This would allow Rich's American doctors to check on him three times a year, in February, June, and September. And it meant we could begin building lives in California, connecting with our new community in San Anselmo and reestablishing ties with family and friends we had seen only sporadically during our long sojourn in Cleveland.

I have often observed that expats who have lived abroad for a long time find it difficult, often impossible, to return to the US. They arrive to find friends and relatives scattered around the country, prices that are outrageous by Seville standards, social and cultural references that mystify them, and a pace of life that's exhausting to the spirit. America is something you have to stay in practice for. We didn't want to lose our touch.

That January, we arrived back in California and officially took possession of the house. Our household furnishings were still en route from Ohio, but the place wasn't completely empty. My sister Kate had arranged to be there to receive the new mattress we'd ordered, and she'd kindly brought over a few things — bedding, a small table, a lamp, some kitchen supplies, a bottle of wine — to make us feel at home. A few days later, the delivery truck arrived with all our belongings.

And when I say "all," I mean "entirely too much." We thought we had been so efficient about getting rid of excess possessions at our garage sale, but we had severely underestimated the size difference between a roomy country Ohio home and a California cottage. As they hauled in furniture and art we'd entirely forgotten we owned, and about two hundred cartons of nik nax, Rich kept saying, "That's about it, right?" And the moving men would just laugh.

By the time they were done our possessions filled the entire house, with boxes stacked from floor to ceiling in the living room and sunporch, leaving only narrow canyons to wriggle through in order to get from one part of the house to another. I called around and found a local storage unit, and we spent the weekend opening every single box and sorting through the contents to determine what to keep out and what to pack away again. Then we hired another moving crew to haul the remaining boxes and furniture away, promising ourselves we would have another garage sale soon.

Our early days in the house involved many trips to the county dump and recycling center, which I believe in hip Marin has some name like the People's Natural Resource Reclamation Cooperative. On one visit, after we'd dropped off yet another pile of flattened cardboard boxes for recycling and were heading for the exit, I was startled to see a flock of peacocks flutter over the car and settle gracefully on a patch of roadside grass to feed.

Clearly Marin had a much classier type of dump than I was used to. When I started to tell my sister about this, I got as far as, "You'll never guess what we saw at the dump today..." And Kate interrupted me to say, "Oh, was it the pig?" There was a pig too? It wasn't a resource reclamation center, it was a zoo.

We soon learned that the epicenter of our new town's social life was a roomy coffeehouse on San Anselmo Avenue, across from the town hall and adjacent to one of the bridges that spanned the creek. An informal atmosphere reigned, with scarred old wooden furniture and an eclectic mix of bicyclists, young families, old hippies, artists, ex-roadies for the Grateful Dead, and once, a guy wheeled in on a hospital gurney, who apparently was in urgent need of some java to speed his recovery. Attire ran the gamut from spandex to jeans to long gauze dresses to pajama bottoms paired with inside-out T-shirts; one elderly woman used to show up wearing a chenille bedspread on her head like a burnoose.

It was comforting to realize that when I become an eccentric old lady wandering the streets in my bathrobe, no one will mind. In fact, when I mentioned this to a neighbor my own age, she said, "But Karen, I do that now!" Good point. Why wait?

We spent five weeks in San Anselmo that winter, organizing the house and getting to know our new community. We flew back to Seville in mid-February, exhausted and ready to enjoy a little of the relaxed Mediterranean lifestyle. When Luz called to invite us to meet the painting group for lunch, we were delighted.

It was one of those perfect, golden afternoons. We ordered platters of ham and roast pork and fried fish, and sipped beer and wine. A street musician serenaded us, and we sang *Bésame Mucho* and danced on the sidewalk to the Anniversary Waltz. As we settled back down in our chairs, we heard cheers and laugher in the street, and looked up to see a bachelor party coming our way. The groom was dressed as a bullfighter, standing on the back footrests of a friend's motor scooter, waving his hat to the crowd. As he swept past us, we realized his costume was nothing more than a printed apron, and he was stark naked from behind. The crowd roared its approval.

I told Rich this was good news for him, because when he becomes an eccentric old man, wandering the streets without his pants, the Sevillanos and the San Anselmans will take it in stride.

In fact, it was good news for both of us. Because in a time of so much change, it was comforting to know we would be able to rely on at least one constant: the steadfast eccentricity of both places we could now call home.

Chapter 10

HEALTH CARE

❧

After the summer of our surgeries, we returned to Spain eager to avoid all doctors and hospitals for a while. This is easy for us to do in Seville; although we have health insurance there in case of emergencies, all our routine medical care takes place in the US. We don't lack confidence in the Spanish system, just in our ability to communicate with it. Accidentally ordering a plate of tripe stew is one thing; it's quite another to say "*Quita la pierna*" (cut off my leg) when you intended to say "*Quita el plato*" (take away my plate of food).

Spain (like all civilized nations) has universal health coverage for its citizens, and the primary care is excellent. First of all — are you sitting down? — they make house calls. All the time. Without a fuss. It's *routine.* The winter after we sold the house in Ohio and bought the cottage in California, I developed a bad case of bronchitis, and after I'd spent four days in bed, Rich phoned our Sevillano health care providers. They said they would send someone out in two hours. Exactly two hours later, a physician showed up at our door carrying his little black bag. I think the last time that happened in the US was during the Eisenhower administration. The doctor examined me right there in my own bed, gave me a diagnosis, prescribed medicine, and departed. No money changed hands; I think they may have done an automatic debit of my bank account for five euros. The medicine worked wonders, and I was back on my feet in a matter of days.

I began to understand why the Spanish live an average of four years longer than Americans, despite the fact that huge numbers of them smoke, drink alcohol (sometimes even at breakfast), and eat vast amounts of ham (which they claim actually lowers cholesterol). I suspect their longevity is due to some combination of the famous Mediterranean diet, the less hard-charging lifestyle, and of course, universal access to medical treatment. Their approach to health care may sometimes appear a little unorthodox by American standards, but it seems to work.

The year before the house call, I consulted a Spanish internist regarding my cholesterol, which had tested a little high just before I left the US. My American physician was recommending a popular cholesterol medication that had perilous potential side effects for the liver, and I wanted a second opinion before I committed to a lifetime on this worrisome drug.

The clinic was about a fifteen-minute walk from my apartment, and I arrived to find a clean, modern facility that was almost shockingly devoid of frills. The waiting room had linoleum floors, plastic chairs, and no magazines or TV screens to entertain the patients. Unlike various bare-bones medical clinics I'd visited in the US, it was not jammed with families toting squalling infants or people who appeared to have been up for days on low-quality recreational drugs. I joined two or three ordinary-looking people sitting calmly on plastic chairs in the quiet room and waited my turn.

Fifteen minutes later my name was called. I went to see my new doctor in a tiny, white-walled office with two chairs and a small desk that held a phone, a boxy desktop computer, and a few folders. I pulled up the only empty chair and sat down.

The doctor was in his late forties, with dark hair and the kind of lined face I always associate with cigarette smokers. He took my medical history himself, and the answers I gave would become part of my universal health record, entered on the computer and stored in my insurance card so that in the future, any Spanish medical practitioner I visited would know about my health issues, treatments, and medications. In the US, where we rely on our memory to fill in countless such forms over a lifetime, we can only dream of the Spanish system's efficiency and accuracy.

My new doctor asked the usual questions: "Do you smoke?" No. "Do you drink?" Yes. "How much?" I was a little startled to add it up; what with all the wine and beer served at lunch and dinner, I confessed that I had about two drinks a day. Where his American counterpart would have immediately handed me a referral for the Betty Ford clinic, this doctor just smiled and said, "Oh, that's nothing. In fact, we have to get that up!" I *think* he was joking.

He ordered a blood test, and two weeks later we met to discuss the results.

"Your cholesterol is a *little* elevated," he said, not sounding too worried about it. "To bring it down, I'd like you to drink more red wine and eat more dark chocolate." I agreed to that rigorous regimen, but if he wanted me to start smoking, I was going to have to draw the line.

I mentioned that I'd heard Spanish ham was also good for lowering cholesterol.

"Yes, it is," he said. "Not all ham, of course." We shared a little chuckle; how silly was *that* notion? "No," he went on, "the only ham that lowers cholesterol is the best ham, *jamón Ibérico*, from pigs that are raised on an acorn diet. You see, because their diet is strictly vegetarian, they do not generate cholesterol. So it is very good for you."

That almost seemed to make sense, until I reflected that other animals — cows, for instance — also have a strictly vegetarian diet, and they're positively bursting with cholesterol. But who was I to argue with my physician? I promised to increase my consumption of *jamón Ibérico*, red wine, and dark chocolate. To hedge my bets, I also started eating oatmeal for breakfast every morning. Eventually my cholesterol levels dropped to the point that there was no more loose talk about liver-threatening medications. Was it the oatmeal, the wine, the chocolate, or the ham that did the trick? Who knows? Who cares? I'm doing my best to consume all of them on a regular basis.

Since then, I haven't had occasion to go back to that internist, nor to call for a home visit from a doctor. But a year after the house call, I caught another horrendous respiratory infection, this one characterized by a deep, persistent cough. From time to time, usually in a crowded shop when I had an armload of purchases, I would feel a small tickle in my throat and before I could fumble for a lozenge, I would be doubled over with huge, wracking coughs that went on and on and on. Grabbing the counter for support, I kept coughing until tears were streaming down my face and the people around me were backing away, clearly wondering if they should be phoning an ambulance, the cops, or a priest to do an exorcism. As soon as I could trust myself to stand upright, I would abandon my purchases on the counter and flee the scene, finishing up my coughing spasm in the relative privacy of the nearest back alley.

This was in December, and with the usual round of holiday parties coming up, I didn't want to risk having this kind of unseemly coughing jag in the middle of a crowded fiesta. The mild homeopathic remedy I keep in my cupboard proved unequal to the task, so I went to the pharmacy in search of some serious drugs. The pharmacist sold me a strong cough syrup guaranteed to do the trick, and I took it home, where I made the mistake of reading the little paper insert that described all the side effects and contraindications. (I am convinced they hire Stephen King to write these things; they're like mini horror movies, with all their talk of dizziness, loss of consciousness, uncontrollable trembling, bleeding from various parts of the body, and death.) I wasn't seriously alarmed until I came to the part that said while taking this medication, you should not consume alcohol, orange juice, or grapefruit juice. I could avoid citrus beverages easily enough, but would I have to refrain from all alcoholic forms of holiday cheer? I went back to the pharmacist, showed him the paper, and asked his advice.

"You *should* avoid alcohol while you are taking this," he said, nodding sagely. "Well, you could have *one* beer. *Two* beers would probably be okay. In fact, you would be fine with *three* beers. But if you really want to..." — he mimed nonstop chugging — "then stop taking the cough medicine."

What a practical solution!

"And drinking orange juice and grapefruit juice?" I asked.

"Stay away from them," he said firmly. "*They* can be harmful."

You have to love a country that feels beer is better for a cold than orange juice.

The Spanish cherish many medical beliefs that you won't find in the annals of the *Journal of the American Medical Association*. For instance, during cold and flu season, I am often advised to place a cut onion beside the bed at night to help clear my sinuses. Somewhat surprisingly, it actually does help, but it isn't going to replace Sudafed any time soon. For general cold symptoms, many Spanish women prescribe garlic, lemon, and honey in herb tea. And the most important health tip of all: never, ever have houseplants in your bedroom, because they can kill you.

Rich and I were totally unaware of our peril, and we could not understand why Luz and Toño got such strange looks on their faces when, as we first showed them around our newly furnished apartment, they saw the bonsais and potted flowers Rich had artfully arranged around the window area of the guest bedroom.

"But, Rich," said Luz, "what do you do with the plants when guests sleep here?"

"Nothing. Why?"

"But everyone knows that plants give off oxygen during the day," she said earnestly, "and they take it in at night. When plants draw in oxygen during the night, they can use up all the air in the room, and the person can't breathe. It can be very, very dangerous."

While I struggled to keep a straight face, Rich, who is a Master Gardener and generally acknowledged as a horticultural expert, tactfully explained why the plants' nocturnal oxygen consumption was so miniscule that it could not possibly affect the air supply of humans in any meaningful way. Luz and Toño weren't buying this for a second. In fact, they thought it was hysterically funny that we were so ignorant about such a basic scientific principle. They would often bring it up at social gatherings; Luz would get a special twinkle in her eye and say,

"Rich, tell us again about houseplants being safe at night." And as Rich painstakingly described the scientific studies he'd looked up on the Internet so that he'd be ready for this question, all the Sevillanos would shake their heads and chuckle. These goofy Americans and their nutty beliefs...

To be fair, the health hazards of houseplants hogging the night oxygen were once commonly feared in the US as well. American friends in their mid-eighties remember similar warnings from their childhoods. Modern scientific research may have torpedoed this notion seventy years ago, but it remains afloat in Andalucía. That's why in Seville, you never bring plants or even cut flowers to a hospital patient. Rich and I know this is all nonsense, of course, and Rich continues his horticultural activities in the spare bedroom. But when our visitors get up in the morning, we always ask them, "How are you feeling today? Any shortness of breath?" So far, we haven't lost a single guest.

Rich and I have been fortunate enough to stay pretty healthy ourselves, and we have rarely had to make use of local medical practitioners. We took out private health insurance when we first arrived, paying what seemed to us the shockingly low cost of $160 a month per person for full inpatient and outpatient coverage, including dental. We continue to carry private insurance, both because the law requires all foreigners to have it and because it gives us access to drop-in clinics that have virtually no waiting time at all.

Rich once had a very minor surgery while we were in the US, and after we returned to Spain, the site became infected. A Seville doctor instructed Rich to stop by the private clinic every day for the next month to have the site cleaned and rebandaged by a nurse. We arrived every afternoon, waiting just the five minutes or so it took to run Rich's card through the computer and generate the paperwork. One day the clinic was unusually crowded, and after we had waited about twenty minutes, we saw a nurse we knew pulling on her coat as she headed out at the end of her shift. She noticed us and came over.

"You are still here?" she said incredulously. "Come with me."

She whisked us into an empty room, shed her coat, washed her hands, put on a gown and gloves, and tended to Rich's infection. Afterwards, she wished us a cheery goodbye and left for the day.

It was an impressive level of service by any standards. And evaluating health care standards is something of a specialty of ours. Rich worked as a hospital administrator for many years and then went on to run vast health systems in California and Cleveland. During my writing career, I had worked as a health writer, health editor, and author of a book on hospitals. Later I served as a consultant to large medical centers seeking to expand services, especially in alternative medicine. For decades, everyone we knew called on us when they were on the brink of hospitalization. We spent so much time in medical waiting rooms and at patients' bedsides that we were jokingly known as the hospital mercenaries, the hired guns you brought in when the going got tough.

When Rich took early retirement in the late 1990s, we began doing volunteer work assignments overseas, often in the health care field. Our first two assignments had us living for months at a time in the former Soviet republic of Georgia, working with clinics struggling to figure out how to make the transition to the new market economy. Ten years after the Soviets' departure and the brutal civil war that followed, Georgia's infrastructure was like a rusty jalopy held together with old coat hangers and duct tape. Most health care facilities were desperately short on heat, electricity, and supplies. Families had to buy all the patients' medications on the black market, which was conveniently located in street stalls in front of the hospital, and latex gloves had to be washed and reused until they wore out altogether. "Don't worry," one of my clients assured me. "If you ever needed serious medical attention, we would arrange for you to fly out to Istanbul." Which was perhaps not quite as comforting as she intended, but good news in its own way.

Arriving in Seville, Rich and I weren't sure what to expect of the health care system; we knew it would be a far cry from the deprivations we'd seen in Georgia, but we'd heard so much about the pitfalls of socialized medicine that we were bracing ourselves for a bureaucratic morass like the one at the *Oficina de Extranjeros*, where we went for our residency cards. Instead, we were pleasantly surprised at the quality and efficiency of care. The clinics might not have the abundance of equipment and amenities common in their American counterparts, but they are modern, clean, and orderly, and treatment is seldom rushed or impersonal. On the few visits we've made to friends in the hospital, we found the staff professional and the atmosphere considerably more tranquil than in US facilities. One American tourist in her seventies, alone and stranded for weeks in the hospital by a sudden illness, became a sort of staff pet; they were all teaching her Spanish to occupy her time and would corral any passing English speakers to pay her a visit.

Every health care system has its weaknesses, and people rightly complain about the drawbacks of the Spanish system. For instance, maternity hospitals assume that your extended family will be on hand to help you with the baby, and if you're an expat alone in your hospital bed with your newborn, you may be seriously shortchanged on the amount of attention and instruction you receive. But overall, Spain has a well-deserved reputation for making good basic care readily accessible to everyone in the community. They have far fewer specialists, however, and you may not be able to find anybody experienced in the more unusual disorders and treatments. If you discover, say, that you'll need a rare form of neurosurgery, you will probably want to consider seeking treatment in another country.

For most of us, the first point of entry into the Spanish health system is the pharmacies. I love going to them. You stand at a little wooden desk and describe your symptoms to everyone within earshot. The pharmacist makes a recommendation, then disappears into the back room, giving the assembled neighbors time to discuss your condition, tell how their Aunt Carmen was a martyr to it, and talk about how their grandparents used to cure it with vinegar, hot salt water, or garlic. If I'm with a friend who has a baby along, everyone feels free to dispense advice about whether the child needs a cap, more blankets, fewer blankets, or adjustments to the clear plastic sheeting that goes over the entire baby carriage, blocking out the air — a common practice in Spain that would be considered child abuse in the States.

When the pharmacist returns with a packet of medication, it usually costs about three euros and works just fine. If you're looking for a simple pain reliever, the pharmacist will sell you a packet of twelve paracetamol for the equivalent of a dollar. When was the last time you bought any American medicine for a dollar?

Not only is the Spanish approach economical, it has a blessed simplicity. In the US, buying even the most basic over-the-counter remedy involves weighing dozens of options. Seeking simple pain relief, you have to sift through the choices of ibuprofen, naproxen, acetaminophen, or basic aspirin, each of which is sold under a bewildering array of brand names, alone or in combination with other ingredients, in various dosages, different shapes and textures, and in regular and childproof containers.

It gives me a headache just thinking about it.

Obviously, the best health remedy is one you don't have to use. While in the US, Rich and I continue to get every kind of checkup our insurance entitles us to; we believe in prevention and catching things early on. Back in Rich's hospital administration days, when everyone we knew was providing medical treatment to everyone else we knew, we heard the same stories over and over again: "He's got *what?* How bad is it? Well, thank God they caught it early. How'd they find it? A routine physical? Figures."

When we were living in Ohio, even basic maintenance seemed to require a calendar studded with medical appointments throughout the year. And let's face it, valuable as they are, actually getting all those tests, diagnoses, and treatments is time-consuming at best, painful and terrifying at worst. Just seeing the word "colonoscopy" on my agenda makes me feel nauseous. One of the unexpected side effects of our living-abroad cycle is that during the eight months of the year I'm in Spain, I almost never see any doctors or dentists at all. Except for the occasional minor emergency, such as my bronchitis, I never even think about medical care. Of course, as soon as I get back to the States I cram in all my appointments as quickly as possible, and that can be a bit hectic. But once that's over, I can relax and enjoy California, and then go back and enjoy my time in Spain.

There's been so much written about the role of stress in causing, exacerbating, and prolonging illness that I can only conclude that anything that reduces stress is good for our well-being. In fact, I now believe that avoiding doctors eight months of the year should be part of everyone's health regimen, right along with dark chocolate, ham, and red wine. Are those things really good for the body? I have an official medical opinion on that, and I am sticking with it. I know for sure that they're good for the soul.

Chapter 11

FESTIVALS

❧

"But what do you *do* all day?" friends from America are always asking.

One of the reasons I love Seville is that nobody who lives here would ever dream of posing such a question. Whether they're working, going to the university, raising kids, on the public dole, retired, or in some less definable situation, the answer most Sevillanos would give is: I just live. But when I try to explain that to my American friends, they find it very unsatisfactory indeed. "But really," they persist, "what do you *do?* How do you fill your *time?"*

It's not hard to fill your time in a city as devoted to public celebrations as Seville. The year is studded with them, like skyrockets exploding one after another, each one so brilliant it eclipses everything else. And the longer I live in Seville, the more I find I am steering the course of my life by these bright lights on the horizon.

By my third year in my adopted city, I noticed that I had begun to define the arrival of spring not by the change in weather, but by the appearance in shops of statues and paintings depicting scenes from Semana Santa (pre-Easter Holy Week). One day the display windows would suddenly include, alongside the usual baguettes or watches or nicotine patches, miniature versions of the grand floats that would soon be carried through the streets, showing scenes from the passion and death of Jesus. The scaled-down figures are complete with the Technicolor gore of the tortured Christ and the Virgin's tears, the tiny lace handkerchief in her hand and the dagger of sorrow piercing her heart. No one seems to find these grisly scenes at all incongruous for selling chocolates or underwear or moisturizing cream.

The next herald of spring is a life-sized robed and hooded figure standing in the entrance of a local shoe store, presiding over a table of polka-dot Mary Janes. The mannequin, recycled from his prior duty as Santa Claus, is now dressed as one of the scary-looking *nazarenos*, the local lay Catholics who march in the processions wearing long, flowing robes and tall, conical headdresses that cover their faces, leaving only narrow slits for the eyes to peer out. Even with Santa's twinkling eyes and wire-rimmed glasses peeking through, the look is distinctly unnerving — as it was intended to be. Designed for medieval penitents marching through the streets in acts of public humiliation, begging God for forgiveness or favors, these creepy outfits were adopted by the equally creepy Ku Klux Klan in the 1860s. Like most Americans, at first I found it impossible to look at the hooded figures without my flesh crawling. By year three I would glance at the one presiding over the shop display and think, "Oh, good, the shoes are on discount, I'll have to mention that to Simone for her girls."

By early March the *nazarenos* are everywhere, including the display windows of bakeries and sweetshops, where little cloth-covered chocolate versions stand in organized ranks, wearing the brotherhood colors that mark the identity of each float and its church as surely as gang colors: purple and white for la Exaltación from the church of Santa Catalina, red and white for Siete Palabras from San Vicente parish, pure black for los Servitas from the chapel of los Dolores. Dropping into a tapas bar on a spring evening, I notice when they switch their TVs from news and sports channels to videos of Semana Santas past, filling the screen with the stately progression of floats and hooded figures and the air with the familiar music — half military march, half funeral dirge — that will soon be the soundtrack of all our lives. In some of the more traditional bars, I see the countdown calendars with rotating numbers that proclaim the number of days remaining until Palm Sunday launches the whole huge, extravagant hullabaloo.

In the run-up to Semana Santa every year, Rich and I often encounter groups of stocky *costaleros* sweating as they practice moving through the narrow streets carrying the bare platforms that will later be weighted down with statues, candles, and flowers. Each night, more cinder blocks are added to their burden until it equals the 2,400 kilos (5,290 pounds) they will carry in the procession itself, each man bearing 60 kilos (132 pounds) of irreplaceable objects of worship on the back of his neck. Just thinking of it always made my spine spasm in sympathy. They are building up their strength for carrying their sacred burden from home church to cathedral to home church again, a journey of eight to fourteen hours. Of course, they'll be setting down the platform frequently to rest, and at intervals the tag team will take over. But even with the lesser burden of the practice platform, I often see sweating *costaleros* ducking out to dash into the nearest bar for a quick beer, and who can blame them?

The final harbinger of spring is the arrival of tourists. In January and February we don't get too many of them, but like the swallows of Capistrano, their spring migration brings them flocking back to the city, where they alight in hotels whose rates have doubled or tripled for the high season. By the eve of Palm Sunday there are a million tourists in town, crowding downtown streets, restaurants, and bars to capacity and refilling the city's coffers after the lean, cold winter months.

Then Semana Santa itself arrives, breaking over the city like a tsunami, sweeping away everything in its path. By midweek, nearly all downtown companies give up any pretense of doing business, monuments shut their doors, schools and gymnasiums close, club activities are suspended, and while markets and bars and cafés remain open, it's often impossible to get to them through the crush of bodies in the streets.

During the first few years I didn't care about any of that, because I was so completely awestruck by the pageantry. Rich and I rushed around with our maps and schedules to catch sight of the various processions, each with their *pasos* (statues) of suffering Jesus and sorrowing Mary accompanied by brass bands, church fathers in splendid vestments, altar boys in velvet and lace, incense bearers swinging burnished censers, and five hundred to twenty-five hundred *nazarenos*, some bearing crosses or walking barefoot or blindfolded as a mark of extra penance.

To add to the drama, the *costaleros* sometimes provide fancy maneuvers, such as coming out of the church on their knees or swaying side to side in a sort of dance at key locations. Locals stand in tightly packed crowds for hours in the hot sun to see these highlights, some weeping with religious fervor, the dense mass of their bodies blocking plazas and roads in every direction. At the periphery of these clusters, the streets are mobbed with locals and tourists roaming from one procession to another, trying to catch glimpses of their favorite *pasos*. The frenzy builds until the culminating hours of Holy Thursday, when traditional Sevillano families get decked out in their best clothes and stay up all night to see the most revered and ancient processions, which move through the streets until dawn in eerie silence, most with *nazarenos* striding along in pure black robes like an army of Darth Vaders, only in some bizarro world where Darth Vader was a Conehead.

Having divine beings in full regalia carried through the streets of the city is dazzling, and I never thought I would tire of it. But by my third year of living in Seville — which meant that, including the prior four years of spring vacations, I'd seen seven Semana Santas — my enthusiasm was on the wane. I began to dread the days when the streets would become impassable, restaurants would be full to overflowing, and most downtown cafés would block off their entrances and set up a bar selling sandwiches and canned drinks to the passing mobs. I braced myself for the days when it would become almost impossible to get into any place offering sit-down meals and a rest room. As a substitute for the latter, our little alleyway is often pressed into service, especially during the late-night processions, creating aromas no amount of incense can mask. Even if I stay inside the apartment, I can hear brass bands playing throughout the day and long into the night.

By my fourth year I was, like so many of my Sevillano and expat friends, rolling my eyes and considering plans for leaving the city altogether.

Instead, I have worked out strategies that let me avoid most of the tumult in the streets. Now I spend the mornings of Semana Santa talking walks and doing errands before the first *pasos* hit the streets around noon. I spend the rest of the day barricaded in the apartment, painting, writing, or doing home improvement projects with Rich. I find I'm actually looking forward to Semana Santa again, but for very different reasons.

But the gravitational pull of something that grand and glorious is hard to resist, and occasionally, when the marching music gets close enough to stir my blood, I put down my paintbrush or close the computer and run downstairs for a look. My favorite moments are at night, when the Virgin sways into view, her face glowing in the light of hundreds of tall white candles. People lean over balcony railings to toss rose petals onto the lacy gold canopy swaying over her head, and occasionally someone will break out into one of the "arrows of song" known as a *saeta* to praise her and thank her for keeping Seville safe during another year. And I remember again all the reasons I love Semana Santa. Still, like the bars with their countdown calendars, I keep my own tally of the days remaining until this wonderful, maddening holiday is over.

By the time Easter rolls around, everyone is exhausted, so thank heavens it's two whole weeks before the next gigantic spring festival.

That would be the Feria de Abril (April Fair), a week-long marathon of all-night drinking and dancing that attracts more than a million people every year. And nearly every woman who goes to the Feria, including me, will show up in one of the *de rigueur*, eye-popping *trajes de flamenca* (flamenco outfits). These are long, skin-tight sheaths that erupt into cascades of enormous ruffles from knee to ankle, in staggering combinations of colors and patterns. I'm talking about lime green with orange polka dots the size of actual oranges, great swirls of red and black trimmed with hot pink, a purple and yellow floral print with purple and red plaid edging — in short, the very colors and patterns your mother told you never, ever to wear together. It's positively shocking. And these outlandish outfits are worn entirely without embarrassment or irony. In fact, when a Sevillana, whatever her age, size, or body shape, puts on her *traje de flamenca*, she knows, right to her bones, that she looks magnificent.

Since my original plan was to be in Seville for only one year, I was reluctant to invest in one of these outfits, which can cost hundreds of euros before you even start adding the mandatory accessories, such as huge, dangling earrings, a fringed scarf, and an oversized fake rose or two for your hair. Luckily, my friend Lynnette is a gifted seamstress who had already made several such outfits for herself, and since we were much the same size, I borrowed one of hers and wore it so often that I eventually persuaded her to sell it to me. It's black with great red roses printed on it, and not only have I worn it every year, but I've loaned it out to numerous expat friends and visitors so they could have a more authentic Feria experience. Even to my untutored eye, the style now looks a trifle dated. Fashions change every year, and the local women can tell from a hundred meters away whether your outfit displays the minute differences in the length, fullness, and arrangement of ruffles, the cut of the neckline, and the set of the sleeves that indicate this year's model. But Rich loves it, and every year he dissuades me from buying another — although he may just be thinking about the hundreds of euros a replacement would cost.

The *trajes de flamenca* evolved from gypsy dresses, which is logical enough, since the fair itself evolved out of the spring horse trading between the gypsies and gentlemen of Seville. In today's Feria de Abril, horseback riders and horse-drawn carriages move leisurely about the fairgrounds all afternoon, stopping at their friends' *casetas* (large tents fitted with a wooden floor, bar, kitchen, and minute bathroom) to have glasses of the traditional *rebujito* (dry sherry mixed with a local soft drink similar to 7Up). My favorite time to go to the Feria is toward sunset; the organizers sensibly prohibit horses there after dark, when the serious drinking commences, and so at the end of the day there's a marvelous impromptu parade toward the exit.

The human revelers return to stay throughout the night, partying enthusiastically, then straggle home around dawn on foot or in the city-subsidized fleet of buses. A few hours' sleep, and they return to the fairgrounds for lunch, more horsing around, and more *rebujitos*. They slip away for a siesta in the afternoon, then come back to dance until dawn. The dancing is a stylized folk dance with flamenco accents, known as the sevillanas, and the locals learn it from the cradle. I've often seen toddlers, portly grandmothers, bartenders, teenagers, and various others spontaneously break out into sevillanas steps in all sorts of settings, from cafés to bus queues. It's surprisingly complex, and I have never mastered its intricacies. I like to watch, though, and I usually spend at least one day at the Feria each year, bedazzled by the vibrant clash of colors and the hardiness of people who can keep up the party night after night for an entire week.

The city often declares the Monday after Feria a holiday known as "hangover Monday," for reasons I probably don't need to spell out for you.

Things do calm down a bit after that, and life settles back into something resembling a normal routine — until the next huge public fiesta, the Pilgrimage of the Rocío, which takes place in May and (thankfully) is held far from Seville. Pilgrimages were popular with medieval Catholics who for various reasons (religious fervor, needing a favor from the Almighty, finding it convenient to get out of town for a while) chose to walk long distances to famous holy places. These *romerías,* as they're called in Spain, enjoyed a huge resurgence during the Franco era, when anticonspiracy laws prohibited Spanish citizens from gathering in groups of more than four unrelated persons unless they received special permission from the police. Church groups were among the few exceptions, so people began signing up for religious road trips, traveling by foot, on horseback, or in ox-drawn carriages, although today, some motorized vehicles bring up the rear of the cavalcade. Three long days and warm nights on the trail in each direction give rise to such shenanigans that one of the local euphemisms for sex is *echar un polvo* (to throw dust). Nine months later there is always a baby boom, and awkward questions about paternity have been known to arise.

The object of the big May pilgrimage is the Virgin del Rocío (Virgin of the Dew), a statue found in a tree trunk back in the thirteenth century. Competing brotherhoods do battle for the honor of carrying the statue out of her church so she can see the sun rise on Pentecost Sunday (fifty days after Easter), a moment that for some reason is so important it draws a million pilgrims every year. People reportedly fling themselves and their babies at the statue in a frenzy of devotion as she is carried through the streets of the little town surrounding the church.

I had heard so much about the Rocío that when Luz offered to show us the town, where a minor event was taking place during the off season, Rich and I jumped at the chance. I went expecting something distinctly posh. The cost of the pilgrimage is considerable; a team of oxen and a flower-bedecked covered wagon can't be cheap, even if you rent them, nor are the women's flamenco dresses (cut a bit looser for all that walking and dust throwing) and the men's short-jacketed suits, leather chaps, and wide-brimmed hats. The journey is also time-consuming, requiring a week to get there and back. In short, the pilgrimage tends to attract the leisured and moneyed class. So I figured the town would be geared to the travelers' every comfort, a sort of Andalucían version of Orlando, Florida.

Instead, we arrived to find what appeared to be the set of a spaghetti western, a town of wide dirt roads and narrow clapboard houses with hitching rails out front. It was like going on a pilgrimage to the OK Corral in Tombstone, Arizona.

"Did ya bring yer six-gun, Tex?" I whispered to Rich.

I was equally nonplussed to see the house owned by Luz's sister, Violeta, and her husband. Where I'd expected something roomy and elegant, I found a cramped, rustic townhouse with a small living room, a skinny downstairs bedroom that barely fit a set of bunk beds for the couple, and an attic where men and women bedded down on mattresses, their clothes tossed over a string hung just below the roof beam.

It struck me that many of Spain's festive occasions are truly meant to be something of an ordeal. The vast machinery of Semana Santa, the Feria, and the Rocío represent an enormous concentration of effort and money, and there's nothing like shared suffering to reinforce that kind of commitment. These festivals hadn't continued for so long *despite* the *costaleros'* backbending labor, the weeks of lost sleep, the crowding and privations of pilgrimage — they continued *because* of them.

That afternoon, jammed into the living room with Luz and Violeta's family and friends, we ate and drank and talked and laughed and watched our hosts dance the sevillanas. And for those few hours, Rich and I had a taste of the sweet sense of belonging that's the payoff for all the hard work and sacrifice it has taken to keep these traditions going for centuries.

Andalucíans pack a huge amount of celebrating into the spring months — I don't even have time to tell you about Corpus Christi, when the streets are fragrant with the scent of rosemary crushed underfoot in the processions, or the Cruz de Mayo tradition of kids building their own mini floats, or the various Virgins who are carried about to bless their barrio. Suffice it to say that by the time summer rolls around, everyone is ready for the enforced rest that the hot weather brings.

Fall in Seville is considerably quieter than the spring. By October, Sevillanos are barely emerging from the summer heat, and with a growing season that rolls on throughout the year for various crops, they've never developed the habit of autumn harvest celebrations. But thanks to Hollywood, Halloween is edging into the culture.

When we first came to live in Seville, there were no Halloween decorations offered in any of the stores. Rich and I hunted all over town for a pumpkin, finally discovering a tiny one in the main department store. Over the next three years, the fad hit town in a big way. Plastic pumpkins and ghost costumes popped up in shops, and little skeletons, bats, and cobwebs materialized among window displays of sweaters and hairbrushes and canned tuna, their gruesome images no more incongruous than the miniature Semana Santa *pasos* that had occupied the space just a few months before. The women's club started holding Halloween costume parties at an Irish pub. Strolling through the Alameda de Hercules, the haunt of the local counterculture, I watched a steady trickle of skeletons, ghosts, and witches flit through the night. Some of the locals, at least, were entering into the spirit of the occasion.

The Spanish get a huge kick out of Halloween and other holiday traditions they've seen in American movies and TV shows.

Most Andalucíans are socially conservative and unlikely to know any Americans, speak any English, or visit the US at any time in their lives, but they are well versed in the Hollywood version of our culture. This leaves them with some very odd notions. For one thing, they are convinced that all Americans are packing firearms and will shoot to kill at the slightest provocation. And they think strange and terrible things inevitably befall innocent travelers driving through America's small towns, such as witnessing a murder and being hunted by the killer; running afoul of local law enforcement officials, drug dealers, or aliens; encountering flesh-eating zombies; or worse. Most Andalucíans wouldn't drive through rural America for any money.

But they are fascinated by Thanksgiving as they've seen it in the movies. Rich, who adores cooking turkey and making mashed potatoes, fixes the full feast for an assortment of Spanish and expats friends every year, and we've recreated the menu on other occasions for groups of Sevillanos who have expressed curiosity about this exotic celebration. Being extremely unadventurous eaters, most Sevillanos don't actually enjoy the food very much, but they appear to be thrilled by such cinematic moments as the presentation and carving of the turkey. The only dish they genuinely like is cranberry sauce, which is nearly impossible to find locally and is usually hand-carried to Seville by expats returning from overseas. Sevillanos' sentiments about Thanksgiving are much like mine about bullfights: it's an enthralling experience but not one they'd like to experience every day, or even every year.

Among the half-learned bits of American culture is the way we celebrate Christmas. The Spanish traditionally gather for a family meal on Christmas Eve, but save the gift giving for Three Kings' Day (Epiphany) on January 6. Nowadays, it's fashionable to give children an additional small gift on Christmas Eve or Christmas

Day, and as you can imagine, the local kids are delighted with the extra loot. Some truly daring Sevillanos are even putting up Christmas trees in their living rooms. They often decorate them like the ones in movie department stores, with matching, evenly spaced ornaments of a single color, a far cry from the motley but beloved collections most American families accrue over a lifetime. So far I've never seen a Spanish tree with a hideous ornament made by a kindergartener out of pasta and old bottle caps, and I think the trees are the poorer for that.

While Christmas trees are not unknown in Seville, buying a good one is still far from easy. Cheap artificial trees from China are readily available in discount stores, but to Rich and me, Christmas isn't the same without a fresh fir like the ones we knew in our childhoods. The few local florists who carry them tend to stock spindly three-foot trees — more like shrubs, really — that come with their roots in balls of dirt and their limbs so dry we can only assume they were dug up well ahead of time, say in June. Even so, we were thrilled to find one at the florist's kiosk in Plaza Alfalfa and carried it home in triumph. Two nights later a windstorm swept through Seville and, due to an open window, right through our apartment as well. In the morning we found our tree sprawled on the floor in a manner so corpse-like, I kept looking for the chalk outline. When we stood it upright, the branches came but the needles — *all* of them — stayed on the floor. It was now just a bundle of dead sticks, like something from *The Nightmare Before Christmas*. We ran out and bought more garlands and wrapped them around the pitiful remnant. With considerable effort and expense, we managed to create something that looked like a lopsided, patchy artificial tree. People kept remarking, "I thought you said you bought a *live* tree."

While decent Christmas trees may be in short supply, Seville is blessed with an abundance of Nativity scenes, from life-sized displays in churches and government buildings to room-sized displays mounted in private homes to little scenes tucked into shop windows. My personal favorites include the all-chocolate Bethlehem in the window of a popular bakery, the deli display showing the Holy Family sheltering under a giant ham, and the army surplus store in which the baby Jesus lies in the manger surrounded by GI Joe dolls in full battle fatigues with rifles, kneeling in reverent homage.

The most popular home decorations are half-life-sized stuffed figures of the Three Kings climbing rope ladders onto apartment balconies to drop off their gifts, giving the general impression the city is being invaded by a swarm of housebreaking Hobbits. The Sevillanos are wild about the African king, Baltasar, whose float serves as the grand finale in the huge parade, known as the Cabalgata, with which Seville celebrates the eve of Three Kings' Day. Whereas American kids visit Santa, Sevillano children come to the department store to sit on Baltasar's lap and whisper in his ear about hoped-for presents.

Among the adult population's most hoped-for holiday presents is, of course, lucky red underwear. To ensure good fortune for the year ahead, red underwear must be received as a gift and worn (discreetly covered by outer clothing, of course) on New Year's Eve. The local shops are full of every conceivable style of red undergarment, including one popular model for men that features the face of an elephant with a huge empty trunk to be filled by the wearer. Rich is never getting one of those in his stocking, I can assure you.

Whatever form of red underwear you are sporting on New Year's Eve, you'll also need to make sure that you have on hand a dozen grapes. Because at precisely midnight, it is customary — no, mandatory — to consume twelve grapes, one at each tolling of the clock; for every one you get down at the right moment, you'll have a month of good luck in the coming year. Eating grapes that fast isn't easy; you have to swallow them whole, and savvy Sevillanos learn early how to peel grapes so they slide more easily down the throat. If you don't want to waste time on New Year's Eve peeling small, slippery fruit, you can buy little cans containing twelve waterlogged grapes for easy chugging. When I asked about the origin of this unusual custom, expecting to hear some story about a saint's miracle or a decree by the legendary King Alfonso the Wise, I was told that back in 1909 the grape growers of Alicante had such a surplus that they came up with this new "tradition" as a way to get the public to take the extras off their hands. It caught on in a big way, and is now as synonymous with New Year's Eve celebrations in Spain as the dropping of the ball in Times Square is in the US.

As you can see, just keeping up with Seville's major holiday traditions is practically a full-time job. Festivals affect every aspect of the city's life, from the economy to how we eat, dress and dance, even the art world. Local galleries are full of paintings of Semana Santa, the Feria and the Rocío. Lots of the Spanish women in my painting classes like to reproduce well-known works based on these popular themes, but busy crowd scenes just aren't my kind of subject. I prefer doing portraits that let me explore the way light plays across a face with enough age and character to throw interesting shadows, and still lifes that show how the sun illuminates the edges of simple objects, such as fruits and vegetables and crockery, with a sort of glorious radiance, like faces of saints in the better sort of old-fashioned paintings.

The Sevillanos respect the fact that I can sell my paintings and are always interested to see what I'm working on. But many remain bewildered that I've left the herd to become an art maverick. Why would I want to paint Karen McCanns when I could be copying the way past masters have portrayed Semana Santa *pasos* or women dancing the sevillanas during the Feria?

My American friends, however, are delighted. At last they can pinpoint something productive in my life. "Oh you *paint*," they say in relief. "*That's* what you do with your time. Why didn't you say so in the first place?"

Chapter 12

CULTURE LAG

❧

When people ask me what I miss most about living in America, I always say it's my family and friends, because of course I do, and besides, if you don't say that, everyone thinks you are totally heartless. But to be perfectly honest, what really springs to mind is how much I miss Saran Wrap. Oh, they have plastic wrap in Spain, but — and I don't mean to shock you — *it doesn't come with a little metal serrated edge for cutting off a piece the desired length.* The cardboard container (so like the US kind in appearance, yet light-years apart in function) has little perforations on the ends that enable you to poke your fingers through and hold the roll of plastic wrap firmly in place with both hands. While doing so, you may invite a friend or relative to pull out the plastic wrap using both their hands, while a third member of the party finds the scissors and cuts a length of film off the roll. By the time I have mustered the personnel and equipment for this task, the half lemon I was planning to wrap has withered, as has my interest in the whole procedure. Nowadays, I try to find recipes that call for complete lemons, and I insist my guests drink enough gin and tonics to use up the entire lime.

Living abroad, the first thing you give up is the ability to go on automatic pilot. Even the simplest daily activities, such as preserving a half lemon or buying basic household tools, require ingenuity and fortitude. One day, when we were first in Seville, Rich wanted to make a small repair in our apartment. After a quick trip to the dictionary, we set out for the hardware store muttering "*destornillador, destornillador, destornillador*" (screwdriver, screwdriver, screwdriver) to ourselves. Unfortunately, when we arrived, my mind went blank and Rich blurted out a similar word, *ordenador* (computer), causing such mutual confusion that we were forced to abandon the attempt and flee the scene without buying either a screwdriver or a computer.

At the time, we were pretty annoyed with ourselves. We felt distinctly foolish, frustrated that a simple errand was thwarted by lack of basic vocabulary and too embarrassed to go back to that particular hardware store anytime soon. But we also got a lot out of the incident: a good laugh, a story we've been telling for years, and — once we ran home and double-checked the dictionary — the word *destornillador* forever etched in our memories.

Unlike those of our friends whose retirement goal is a life of untrammeled ease, I like facing up to the challenges of life in a new country. It adds a lot of zest to the daily round. When a simple visit to the hardware store becomes a test of skill and wit, I know that even if I walk away without a screwdriver, at least I am acquiring the tools I need to keep my brain — and my sense of humor — ever more finely honed. "There are good days, and there are bad days, and this is one of them," Lawrence Welk is said to have remarked, and that is the essence of expat life.

Traveling back and forth between two countries twice a year, I have lots of Lawrence Welk days. Not only do I cross nine time zones each way, I step off the plane into very different versions of reality. Returning to my native land after just four months of living in a foreign country is surprisingly disorienting. While it's easy to slip back into my mother tongue, it's tougher to let go of my Sevillano lifestyle and pick up all the threads of my American life. I always discover a bewildering array of unexpected changes in the social, political, economic, and cultural scene — to say nothing of whatever family dramas are going on. Even things that have stayed more or less the same *seem* different when I see them with the fresh eyes of a new arrival. What's taken for granted — what *defines* words like "normal" and "home" — changes so abruptly, I get culture lag.

Many cultural differences are delightful. Arriving at our San Anselmo cottage, I thrill to such unaccustomed luxuries as central heating and air conditioning, a clothes dryer, a dishwasher, a TV, a garbage disposal, and Saran Wrap with a serrated metal cutting edge right on the box. After the low-budget Ikea furniture we bought for our Spanish apartment, the comfy Pottery Barn sofa and our midcentury overstuffed armchairs seem positively opulent. Old familiars, such as my parents' cigarette table and the etchings that once graced the walls of Rich's childhood home, feel like surreal relics of an unimaginably distant past, possibly on another planet.

The house always appears fresh and welcoming, thanks to a housekeeper who comes in before we arrive to remove the dust sheets from the sunporch and clean and air out the house. We don't bring much in our carry-on luggage, since we maintain wardrobes and the essentials of life in both places, so it doesn't take us long to unpack. When it's time to put the suitcases away, Rich opens the ceiling hatch and draws down the folding ladder that leads to the attic. And I marvel once again at the perfection of design that positioned this steep, rickety, swaying ladder so that anyone who took a tumble down it would be able to continue unimpeded all the way down the main staircase, bank once on the turn, roll across the tiny foyer, fly right out the front door and somersault down six more steps to the front walk. You just don't get engineering like that anymore.

Once we've safely stowed our bags away, Rich and I take a walk around town to stretch our legs and see what changes have taken place in our absence. We usually arrive in midafternoon, having spent the previous night in London so as to catch the morning nonstop flight to San Francisco. After ten straight hours on the plane, watching movie after movie, the walk clears our heads and helps us feel a bit more grounded.

Our cottage is behind the town hall, library, and police station, around the corner from the sleepy main street, and our leisurely stroll takes us past modest houses and low apartment complexes to the town's small businesses, shops, and restaurants. After the bustle of Seville, with its crowded sidewalk cafés and hordes of shoppers and tourists, walking along the wide, nearly empty sidewalks of San Anselmo seems strange — somehow both lonely and peaceful. Where Sevillanos like to gather frequently in public places, reveling in the vibrant hum of boisterous conversation, San Anselmans spend much more time at home, in their cars, or at work. But when they do want company, they often gather in the roomy coffeehouse situated on the town's main street beside the creek that meanders through town on its way to San Francisco Bay.

With all the other changes in our lives and in the world, I find it tremendously reassuring to arrive at that coffeehouse time and again to see what appear to be the same dogs and bicycles parked outside. Going inside I like finding the familiar battered old wooden chairs and the usual mix of customers: gray-bearded men with Hawaiian shirts and long ponytails, spandex-clad cyclists, women in yoga pants, children sporting everything from Ralph Lauren sweaters to homemade tie-dyed T-shirts, men and women in city suits, and an artist named Michael, who has a kiosk down the street and is as much a fixture in the coffeehouse as the espresso machine.

On our winter visits, we often stroll outside with our coffee to check out the water level in the creek. Normally it meanders along cheerfully at the bottom of a deep, leafy cleft, looking about as threatening as a chocolate muffin. But every twenty years or so, when an especially heavy winter rainfall coincides with an incoming tide, the creek rises fast, overflows the storm drains, and pours through the downtown streets — including ours — in a waist-high torrent of muddy water and debris. (Yes, we knew this when we bought the house; hence the flood insurance.) Luckily for us, some years ago our house was raised up just high enough to let the floodwater swirl harmlessly beneath the floorboards — unless some year, in these times of global climate change, it manages to rise just a few inches higher. Three days after we moved into the San Anselmo house, the creek came to within an inch of overflowing, and two years later it swelled alarmingly, but so far we've missed all the action.

After checking out the coffeehouse and the creek level, Rich and I usually wind up our reentry walk with a trip to the grocery store for supplies. And that's where the culture lag really hits me: right in the cereal aisle.

I'm used to Seville's "supermarkets," which offer maybe a dozen cold cereals, eight of them chocolate, which considerably streamlines the decision-making process. If I want something as outlandish as oatmeal, I have to go to a health food or department store. But when I arrive in a California supermarket,

I'm confronted with an aisle as long as a cathedral's displaying hundreds of kinds of cold cereal and several shelves of hot varieties. There are a dozen types of oatmeal alone: instant, quick, old-fashioned, organic, steel-cut, rolled, Scottish, Irish, spice-maple, apple-cinnamon, raisin-date-walnut, peaches and cream, strawberry, boxed, bagged, bulk... At about this point the room begins to swoop and spin around me, and I grab the simplest thing I can find and flee.

The produce aisles are equally mind-boggling. After months of shopping in Seville, where fruits and vegetables are modest and seasonal — and in the small barrio "supermarkets," often elderly, bruised, and battered — the California fruits and vegetables seem like movie stars: so big and gorgeous and bursting with vitality, it's hard to believe they're real. I often wander aimlessly about just caressing the red peppers and sniffing the fresh dill, until I finally pull myself together and make some purchasing decisions so we can go home.

It takes me about a week to adjust to the time difference. The first few nights I struggle mightily to stay awake past eight and often find myself up again at four or five in the morning. Where this would be monstrously out of step with the pace of life in Seville, among Californians, it's considered normal. I have many friends and relatives who rise at five every day so they can get in an early morning run or beat the commuter traffic to work. In a way, I'm lucky that insomnia and jet lag get me out of bed at such an appropriate hour by local standards.

In California, *all* the activities of daily living, and most especially eating, sleeping, and socializing, occur at wildly different times than they do in Seville. Few Sevillanos are about at six o'clock in the morning unless they're wending their way home after a late night; you won't find them, like their San

Anselmo counterparts, voluntarily getting up at that hour just to get a jump on the day. Americans don't eat a second breakfast at ten, so they are starving for lunch by noon, often eating a sandwich at their desks so they can devote more time to work. The Sevillano dines leisurely at two, and many business people and blue-collar workers alike enjoy a hot three-course meal with beer or wine.

When in Seville, Rich and I often have a half pint of beer with lunch; after all, we're not driving, operating heavy equipment, or doing anything more hazardous than walking home through busy streets to take a siesta. In California, however, we quickly dropped the habit, since we became rather self-conscious about people staring at us throughout the meal, clearly trying to figure out whether they should give us a card for the local chapter of AA or contact our families about organizing an intervention.

When we go out in the evenings, I have to remind myself not to gasp over the prices. I'm staggered to see wine at fourteen dollars a glass when I'm used to paying eight for a bottle at a good restaurant. With Seville's recession-conscious bars reducing the cost of small bottles of beer to about a dollar apiece, I sometimes forget myself enough to blurt out, upon reading a California menu, "*Five-fifty* for a beer?" Only to have our friends reply, "Yes, aren't the prices here *great?*"

Of course, one of the biggest differences in the two cultures is the attitude toward siestas. While they are still standard in Seville, with nearly all shops and businesses closing from two to five every afternoon, in the US sleeping after lunch is regarded as a sign of eccentricity and/or weakness. Americans often refer to our siestas as "naps," as if we were four, or ninety, or just hopeless slackers. When we're in California we make every effort to keep taking siestas, but the culture conspires against us: maintenance workers arrive at one and settle in for hours, delivery people keep ringing the doorbell, appointments have to be scheduled in the early afternoon to accommodate the doctor's availability, and so on. And there's not much point in taking a late siesta after all these interruptions cease, because by five o'clock, it's nearly dinnertime.

We have often been invited out for the evening and told to meet at the restaurant at five thirty. And we're not talking about grabbing the early-bird special at a greasy spoon, but fine dining at an upmarket restaurant. We often go out for a night on the town and arrive back home by eight thirty, enabling our friends, who have been up working hard since five, to get to bed at a "reasonable" hour. Fresh from Seville, where we go out for the evening at nine, Rich and I find the idea of such an early bedtime disorienting. Apparently we are alone in this, because if we're out "late" — say, coming back from a movie in the next town at nine thirty — we find San Anselmo's main street dark, with the few restaurants that are still open ushering out the last customers and turning off the lights.

Is it any wonder I suffer from culture lag?

Rich moves back and forth between our two lives with the ease of a man strolling from one room to another in his own house. I find the transitions much more difficult. Spending the majority of my time in Seville, I get deeply attached to my circle of friends and the rhythm of my life there. Arriving in California, especially in the first two or three years after we bought our cottage there, I often felt unsettled and off balance, as if the sturdy floor beneath my feet were shifting like a ship's deck in a high sea. Some of the very cornerstones of the American lifestyle seemed alien to me, and none more so than driving.

Growing up, I couldn't wait for the freedom represented by a driver's license, and during my adult life I'd spent countless hours behind the wheel without a second thought. But after four years in Seville and two of owning a home in San Anselmo, I discovered that I'd gotten used to life at a pedestrian's pace and found the noise of driving, the rattling speed, and the split-second, life-or-death decisions distinctly unnerving. On top of everything else, we'd sold my old car right after selling the Cleveland house, so our only transportation was Rich's beloved PT Cruiser, a stylish but cumbersome vehicle with poor visibility and a stick shift. Rich likes to really engage with a car; I just want it to take me where I'm going without a lot of back talk. I found myself driving less and less, perhaps a dozen times a year at most, which meant I never got comfortable with the car or the routes and spent a great deal of time getting horribly lost, grinding gears and my teeth in frustration.

One of the reasons I could drive so rarely is that our San Anselmo home is walking distance from nearly all the essentials of life: markets, restaurants, shops, movies, the public library, art supply stores, yoga classes, and huge parks with lakes and trails. But there is one exception: most of my close friends and family aren't all that close, geographically speaking, and just meeting for lunch or dinner often entails hours on the freeway. Rich loves to drive and is happy to zip us about the Bay Area. But when we'd been living in San Anselmo for a couple of years, I realized I was making elaborate efforts to avoid any social commitment for which I'd have to drive long distances solo. This severely restricted my ability to meet up on my own with old friends and most of my relatives. I knew few people in San Anselmo itself, and cultivating new friendships was severely hampered by the fact that I was always leaving again so soon.

During those first years in San Anselmo I often felt distinctly alienated from my home culture. There was too much driving, too few siestas, too many people rushing around at dawn trying to squeeze in more time for work. It made my nerves jangle. I missed the easy spontaneity of friends like Simone and L-F ringing my doorbell to invite me out for coffee, leisurely evenings with my Irish pal Molly in a tapas bar, wandering around some obscure Andalucían town with Luz and Toño. I missed lunches that lasted five hours and breakfasts with old men lingering over their *fino* in the corner.

Finally, during my third summer in San Anselmo, it occurred to me that I was fixated on viewing California not as it was, but through the lens of my life in Spain. While the rest of me was arriving in San Anselmo, I'd left my head and heart back in Seville. I was not mentally unpacking my bags. Despite living just a short distance from the communities in which I grew up, went to college, got married, and had family all over the place, I felt more like a foreigner than I did in Spain — or Cleveland, or Boston, or any of the other places I'd lived. In California I had great relationships with lots of individuals, but I felt disconnected from the larger community.

It took me a long time to come to this realization, and even longer to begin understanding why. I had arrived assuming I knew the place; after all, I'd lived in California off and on throughout my life and visited often during the years when I made my home elsewhere. I wasn't looking at it with fresh eyes, as I would any truly new place. T. S. Eliot's famous lines from *Four Quartets* — "We shall not cease from exploration / And the end of all our exploring / Will be to arrive where we started / And know the place for the first time" — did not seem to apply to me. I was investing less in California, and expecting more from it, than I would any other place on the planet.

I was still pondering this new insight when the local arts council invited me to put up an exhibition of my paintings at the main coffeehouse in San Anselmo. I thought it would be a great excuse for a party and with luck, even in the tough art market following the global economic recession, I might manage to sell a painting or two. So I set a date for the opening night party, put up posters all over town, sent out notices to everyone on my email list and reminded all the neighbors that the coffee bar had just gotten its wine and beer license and it was in our best interests to support it.

The opening was on an August night so hot that all the helium balloons I'd tied up out front exploded one by one. But even without balloons to mark the spot, people found it and came pouring in: my family, old friends, new friends, neighbors, fellow artists, people I hadn't seen since high school, a couple I'd met in Seville, my hairdresser, my doctor, Rich's old navy pals, the coffeehouse regulars, a couple of homeless guys who'd heard there was free food. Looking around the room, listening to the heady buzz of conversation and laughter and my brother Steve's mellow guitar playing, I realized that I really *had* been blind to what was going on around me. I was in a room full of great people who cared about me; I *did* have a community, and I *did* belong there.

And on top of all that, I sold four paintings.

Today, I am relearning the lost art of being engaged in California culture. When I'm there, I drive more, siesta less and try not to complain about the restaurants in San Anselmo closing their kitchens at eight thirty. I realize that even friends who live an hour away and require two weeks advance notice for lunch *are* part of my social circle, the network of people who give my life substance, make me laugh and let me know that I am loved.

My reentries in both directions are much smoother now, although I don't know if I'll ever achieve Rich's sublime insouciance about them. We replaced the PT Cruiser with a zippy little red VW with an automatic transmission and a GPS system that takes a lot of the stress out of driving. A great Mexican restaurant opened in San Anselmo that actually stays open until midnight, so we finally have someplace to go after the movies. I make sure I have sufficient projects, such as writing this book, working on my blog, and painting, to keep me happily occupied wherever I am. And I make sure that every stay in California includes plenty of time with the people I care about, even if it means hours of solo driving on the freeways.

Our time in California starts with a round of welcome-home gatherings, and before I know it, we're meeting for farewell dinners on the eve of another departure for Seville. It is really hard to say so many goodbyes, especially to those who are so old or ill that I fear I may not see them again. Emails and phone calls, even with Skype video, simply aren't the same as being there, although they help me keep tabs on the news and gossip so I will be up to speed when I see my stateside friends and family again in four months.

Or sooner. One of the great things about living in a destination city like Seville is that people make every effort to come to you. In an era when airfares are so low that you can fly from one European city to another for less than a round of drinks in a San Francisco bar, people are always saying, "We're going to be in Paris, so we thought we'd drop by and see you." What's nine hundred miles between friends?

Which brings me to the subject of the next chapter: guests.

Chapter 13

GUESTS

❧

"I tell everyone who moves here: get a one-bedroom place," a Belgian expat said during my first visit to southern Spain. "Otherwise people will expect to stay with you." What was wrong with that, I wondered; it's fun to entertain guests.

How naive I was back then! Of course, I'd been living for a long time just outside Cleveland, which isn't exactly a destination city, and we'd had relatively few house guests during those years. As my sister Melissa explained, "I just can't bring myself to call up a San Francisco travel agent and tell her I'm taking my family to Cleveland for vacation." Those who did visit us always seemed pleasantly surprised — stunned, even. When my brother Mike flew in from Silicon Valley, he kept saying, "But this is really quite *nice*," in a bemused sort of tone, as if he'd expected to find us living in a trailer park between a smokestack and a slag heap.

However, living in a tourist destination like Seville, I soon found that my guests arrived with considerably higher expectations. Early on, a British expat explained to me that you have to set boundaries right from the start. "When people want to visit me," he said, "I always tell them the rules: You can come for three days, no more, and during that time you will take me out for a nice meal at a restaurant of my choosing. And I don't do airport transport." It all sounded so cold and harsh; I couldn't imagine treating my guests that way.

Now, after living six and a half years in Seville and entertaining upwards of a hundred visitors — although to be fair, some did stay in nearby hotels instead of our apartment — I realize the expat community was passing on valuable survival tips. Of course, by then it was far too late for us; we had already rented a three-bedroom place and told everyone we knew to look us up if they ever came to Seville. And they did.

Let me hasten to say that most of our guests have been perfectly delightful, embracing their brief stay in Seville with enthusiasm, enjoying the rich cultural offerings of the city, amusing us with lively conversation, bringing the latest news and gossip from the old country, and being considerate of our time and resources in every possible way. In some, however, we have not been quite so fortunate. We've hosted couples whose relationship was spinning out of control and had reached the bitterly acrimonious stage, people whose mood-altering medications had recently been adjusted in unfortunate ways, families in shock from ghastly visits with in-laws, the elderly who were sliding fast into senility, businesspeople in the throes of a career crisis, parents whose children were undergoing emergency medical treatment back home, and so on. With their lives in that kind of turmoil, these troubled souls naturally had little attention to spare for the people and places around them and couldn't be expected to contribute to the general joie de vivre. And they didn't.

Then there are the teenagers. As you have no doubt observed, some teens go through a sullen phase, and such kids arrive in

Seville acting as if they have been dragged to Europe at gunpoint. Monosyllabic responses, eye rolling, and hunched shoulders eloquently indicate that they are way too hip to be traveling with these total losers. They sleep until noon, and when they finally drag themselves out of our apartment at two o'clock, they are deeply affronted to find everything closed for siesta. They are disgusted that the locals don't speak English. They couldn't possibly try the food. There's nothing to do. Their only recourse is to sink further into resentful silence and wait morosely until they get back home, where they can consort with people who are as mature and hip as they are.

My Irish friend Molly sits such teenagers down when they arrive and explains that in her house, they are expected to keep up their end of the conversation, and if they can't do that, they should find another place to stay. My sister Melissa used to fine her children a dollar if they used an incomplete sentence. I have never summoned the nerve to try either of these approaches, but I admire their spirit and hope someday to work my way up to implementing them.

Not every teenager who shows up at our place is grumpy and alienated. Many are delightful company, enthusiastic about being in Spain and eager to experience local culture. And the local culture they're most eager to experience is, of course, the teenage bar scene. Here in Seville, the drinking age is sixteen, and kids as young as fourteen may be served if they're not too baby-faced. It's not uncommon for local teens to head out at midnight and frequent youth bars and *botellones* until dawn. To most American kids, who have been raised with the understanding that they will not experience this kind of night on the town until they turn twenty-one, if ever, the idea that it could happen to them ¡here, tonight! is heady stuff.

Their parents are naturally less thrilled at the prospect. Families usually spend the first evening they're in Seville negotiating this point. The parents start out using phrases such as "over my dead body" and "maybe when you're thirty," but kids are experts at wheedling and bargaining, and the force of their arguments is given weight by sheer persistence. As parental resistance begins to crumble, everyone turns to us and asks what we think the kids should be allowed to do.

This is one question Rich and I refuse to answer. Naturally we want the kids to have a great time and, if possible, a few memorable adventures to brag about back home. Seville is a safe city; aside from the occasional purse snatching, crime is rare, and the *botellones* are unlikely to result in anything more than a brief scuffle. But it is a city, and anything can happen. We don't want to be responsible for sending inexperienced kids who speak about five words of Spanish out on their own late at night to fend for themselves in a foreign urban environment. At best, they are likely to lose their cell phones and maps and wind up calling us from a pay phone at three in the morning to come get them. At worst… we've all read the headlines.

Left to decide for themselves, the parents usually yield in the end and allow the teenagers go out, but only if they *give their word* that they will not drink any alcoholic beverages, that they will stick together the whole time, and that they will be home by three in the morning. The kids all nod solemnly and swear to everything and anything so long as they are allowed out that door into the wonderland that they are sure awaits them. They then find the nearest youth bar, have a rum and Coke, split up and go their separate ways, have a few more rum and Cokes with newfound friends at different bars, and stagger home about three, eating handfuls of peppermint along the way. In the morning, the parents always assure us that the kids didn't have a single drink, they just walked around admiring the local culture. And I always say, "Yes, the cathedral is lovely in the moonlight," and pretend to believe this is what happened.

The first morning of the visit, we usually take our houseguests (minus any teens who are home sleeping it off) to our favorite café for breakfast and a discussion of plans for their stay. To be perfectly honest (although we try to put this more tactfully to our guests), what we usually want to do is give them an orientation tour of Seville, a map, and a latchkey, and then send them off on their own, with plans to meet up later. It's not that we don't want to spend time with them, nor do we mind visiting the cathedral or the Alcazar palace for the twenty-fifth time; they really *are* worth seeing over and over again. However, we have full lives of our own in Seville and often have projects and obligations calling for our attention. Sometimes it's very awkward for us to drop everything — for instance, finishing a painting for an upcoming show or shopping for a sick friend — to take guests sightseeing. We naturally want to spend time with them — just not twenty-four hours a day, especially during longer visits.

But some guests assume we'll do just that, and they are deeply wounded and/or terrified if we suggest anything less. These guests get up every morning and ask, "What are we doing today?" If I inquire what they'd like to do, they reply, "You decide. You know the city better than we do." If I propose a little exploring on their own, they protest, "But we might get lost. And besides, we don't speak Spanish." If I offer these guests a map, a phrase book, and directions to the café two blocks from our front door, they look at me as if they're dangling off a cliff and I'm Wile E. Coyote sawing away at their rope. If they really can't cope with the city on their own, Rich and I give in gracefully and rearrange our schedules to make ourselves available throughout their stay. We endeavor to be good hosts, even on those occasions when, as the saying goes, "Hospitality is making your guests feel at home, even though you wish they were."

Occasionally this has backfired horribly. Twice we've had houseguests come for a weekend and stay for nearly two weeks, demanding full-time guest services every day. They kept saying blithely, "I know we planned to go on to Cordoba, Ronda, and Granada, but you're just making us so comfortable, we simply can't bear to tear ourselves away! You don't mind if we stay another few days, do you? This is such fun!"

What could we do? The rules of hospitality prevented us from chucking them bodily out into the street. Besides, these were friends of long standing; we might actually want to see them again. So we just kept pointing out the attractions of Cordoba, Ronda, and Granada, printing out information about charming hotels in other parts of Andalucía, and bringing home train schedules and car rental brochures. The friends kept talking about leaving in a day or two or three. In the end, they stayed on in our apartment until it was time for their return flights back to the States. And we suspect they wouldn't have left even then if their airline tickets hadn't been nonrefundable.

And then, every once in a while, there's a visit that somehow, magically, against all odds, goes spectacularly right. One in particular stands out. It was during Semana Santa, which the expat community universally considers the grisliest of entertaining nightmares. The relentless crowding and craziness, the ghoulish imagery, the constant charging about in search of the next *paso*, all make Holy Week an ordeal that is daunting for even the most seasoned traveler. Our guests have been known to collapse in exhaustion after the first day and refuse to leave our apartment until after Easter.

But this one California couple not only had the hardiness and good humor required to endure the rigors of Semana Santa, but was blessed with the most astonishing amount of sheer good luck we'd ever seen.

Everything about the visit went right. Although they had just been staying in five-star hotels, they managed to convince us they were charmed by the modest comforts of our guest room and adored everything about our apartment. When we stepped out into the streets, they were unfazed by the human traffic jam and soldiered on cheerfully in Rich's wake as he found a nearby procession. By some miracle we arrived just in time to see a gorgeous, weeping Virgin surrounded by a sea of white roses, her tasseled awning swaying, the brass band in her entourage playing a rousing tune. After watching a hundred of her trailing *nazarenos* march past, we ambled over a few blocks and found the perfect viewing spot just in time to see a different procession's *paso* of Jesus at the whipping post. As it passed us, the *costaleros* made the platform do a special sort of swaying maneuver for the crowd, to enthusiastic applause.

By now it was getting hot, and just as the thought of a nice, cold beer drifted across our minds, we spotted a table opening up at one of our favorite sidewalk cafés. After a refreshing break and lively conversation, we heard another band and strolled over to catch another procession, naturally arriving just as someone began singing a *saeta* to the Virgin. It went on like this for two days.

On the third morning, as we were sitting at a sidewalk café having coffee before our guests took their departure, one of them mentioned that he was fascinated by the tunes the bands had been playing. I glanced over and, naturally, there was a newspaper stand a few yards away selling CDs of Semana Santa music.

It seemed nothing could go wrong. We were sorry to see our friends go; not only had the visit been great fun, but we kept hoping some of their good luck would rub off on us.

As we watched their rental car disappear into the traffic jam encircling the city, I said to Rich, "That visit certainly worked out well."

"I had a *great* time," he said. "In fact, I can't help wondering why we don't entertain house guests more often."

Chapter 14

SNIFFING THE AZAHAR

❧

Nowadays, when guests come to visit, one of the first places I always take them is quite possibly the most hideous site ever built in Seville: the giant mushrooms in the Plaza de la Encarnación.

When I first arrived in Seville, this downtown plaza was just a city-block-sized hole in the ground. And we all thought *that* was an eyesore!

The debacle began with the bright idea of adding an underground garage below what had been a farmers' market for more than 150 years. As is so often the case in Seville, the moment the first shovel broke ground, workers unearthed a treasure trove of Roman, Moorish, and Visigoth ruins. The construction project was put on hold and remained stalled for the next thirty-seven years.

The farmers, fishermen, and butchers who'd made their living in the market spent those years crowded into "temporary" quarters at the edge of the plaza. And while underfunded archeologists toiled to preserve the most important artifacts, city leaders developed ever more grandiose ideas for the site. It was to be more than a market, it would become a monument; no, a world-famous icon like the Guggenheim Museum in Bilbao, the Eiffel Tower, the pyramids of Egypt...

When I first saw the faded architectural drawings posted near the site, I was astounded that even a city government committee could approve something that was at once so ugly, so useless, and so stunningly expensive.

The design involves six irregularly spaced towers, each a hundred feet high and topped with what look like amoeba-shaped, open-weave waffles that provide little protection from sun or rain. The impression is enough like gigantic, interlocking toadstools that they inevitably became known as the *setas* (mushrooms). The styling of the *setas* is pure 1960s, so much like the overblown set of some pseudo-hip sex comedy from that era that I keep expecting to see Peter Sellers and David Niven grooving under the magic mushrooms in Nehru jackets.

But ghastly as the *setas* are, as soon as they opened last year, everyone flocked to them. The plaza is a perfect rendezvous point, being centrally located and impossible to miss. And it does have some cool features. I often take visitors to the subterranean *antiquarium* — or ANTIQVARIVM, as the sign puts it, to emphasize the fact that there are ROMAN RVINS down there. The dimly lit space artfully displays the remains of ancient foundation stones and reconstructed mosaic floors, along with smaller artifacts that somehow failed to find their way into the archeological museum or onto the black market. After the ANTIQVARIVM, I always suggest to visitors that we hop in the elevator to the skywalk and check out the view, a sweeping vista of the city's rooftops and church towers, to say nothing of glimpses into the windows of nearby apartments. After that, we usually refresh ourselves at the one place in the complex that truly *was* a stroke of genius: a ground-level café offering a bucket of five mini beers in a bed of ice for a mere three euros. This instantly became the most popular spot in town, and even the harshest critics had to admit that the *setas* look a lot more attractive after a bucket of beer.

The people who commissioned the Metropol Parasol Building (as it's properly called) fondly believe that it will become a world icon, an architectural landmark, and a major tourist attraction for generations to come; but others, including me, remain skeptical. For one thing, the amorphous shape doesn't translate well to a logo suitable for souvenirs; people back home won't look at your new refrigerator magnet and think you went to Seville, they'll think you went to a science exhibit on amoebas. And the *setas* have the distinction of being the largest wooden structure in the world *and* the largest structure ever held together with glue, and neither of those materials tends to hold up at all well in Seville's blistering summer heat. Those who consider the complex a blight on the architectural landscape are waiting in happy expectation of watching it crumble away in the coming years. Its supporters insist the wood's vinyl cladding and extra-strong superglue will hold the structure together, and they're waiting in happy expectation of proving the detractors wrong. The rest of the populace is waiting in happy expectation of the next bucket of beer.

Ambitious architectural projects often spark this kind of controversy, and I'm sure fifteenth-century Sevillanos responded in much the same way to the construction of what was, at the time, the largest cathedral in the world. Detractors who criticized the design were quickly proved to have a point: just five years after construction was finished, the cathedral's dome collapsed and had to be rebuilt several times. But Sevillanos have always had more optimism than common sense. And I have to give them credit. It isn't easy for a city so rooted in the past to make such a bold statement about the future, even if that statement tends to stutter and the future they're embracing is already half a century in the past.

But then, when you live in city that deals so casually with centuries and millennia, the whole concept of time is different. Memories are long in Seville. Spanish friends are always gossiping about some nefarious scheme cooked up by the archbishop and the mayor, and when I am puzzled because I don't remember seeing anything about it in the newspaper, they kindly explain that it happened in 1397. Oh, *that* graft scandal.

One afternoon I was sitting in my favorite café with Lindsay, an American friend soon to be married to a Spaniard, talking about Sundays. Here, virtually all shops and businesses are closed on Sundays, and it's a given that families gather for a long lunch together. American women who adore their Sevillano boyfriends or husbands often find this a sticking point. "*Every* Sunday?" they ask, staggered by the enormity of the revelation. "We have to eat with your parents and brothers and sisters every Sunday *for the rest of our lives?*" Lindsay was fortunate enough to escape this fate, since she was marrying into a somewhat bohemian Spanish family, what with her future father-in-law living off the grid and her future mother-in-law being a sex therapist. As I was congratulating her on her good luck in the in-law department, we heard a considerable amount of commotion in the street and went out to take a look.

A huge procession was heading our way, with a life-sized statue of the Virgin, hundreds of candles, thousands of flowers, clouds of incense, dozens of people in sixteenth-century robes, and a band playing boisterous religious marching music. After it had passed, Lindsay and I had barely settled back into our seats when we heard more noise and jumped up to see a wedding party approaching, the bride and groom sitting in a beribboned, flower-bedecked, horse-drawn carriage, waving to the cheering crowd as if this were the closing scene of a Merchant Ivory film. A few minutes behind them, a motorcycle gang roared into view — thirty tough-looking hombres in full leathers, revving their engines and cutting a swath through town.

Lindsay and I agreed you have to love a town where you never know what century is going to be coming around the corner at you.

Seville is a city of so many centuries, layers, and cultures, I'll never be able to explore them all. I've had guests who spent three days here and announced they had plumbed the depths of the Seville experience and were ready to move on. I, on the other hand, have known the city for more than a decade and am still surprised by it nearly every day. I am amazed by what disappears (the pet store that used to sell squirrels and chipmunks, for example — go figure!) and what keeps on, year after year.

One thing that has remained steadfastly in place, in the very shadow of the new *setas* in Plaza de la Encarnación, is the little old gypsy woman who sells wild asparagus and live snails off a wooden crate on the sidewalk. I admire the woman's enterprise, but I'm always distressed watching the poor snails practically extruding themselves from their shells in their desperation to get out of the mesh bag. One day, as I walked past her crate, I glanced down at the ground and discovered that a single snail had somehow worked its way free. It was two meters away and was proceeding along the sidewalk with all the fierce determination and speed of which a snail is capable. I wanted to cheer out loud for it; instead I silently wished it well and went on with my day, scarcely remembering to mention the incident to Rich.

Fast forward to Christmas morning, when I discovered a small orange box under the tree. On it was a note that read, "What do we want? Freedom. When do we want it? Now!" Mystified, I opened it up.

Inside were two brown snails.

"I got them from the old gypsy woman," Rich said. "It's like the pardoning of the turkeys at Thanksgiving. How many people get to save a life at the holidays?"

How many indeed? And I was twice blessed.

I named the snails Churro (for the golden curls of fried dough so popular here) and Chocolate (for the thick hot drink that you dip your churros into). Later that day Rich and I carried them down to a nice patch of grass by the river. Churro and Chocolate just lay there, either stunned by their good fortune or perhaps too dehydrated to move after hours in the little orange box. Rich assured me they would be fine and that there was every chance they would live out happy lives in the tall grass, evading any attempts by the old gypsy woman to recapture them for the Sevillanos' dining table.

Like the snails, I am hoping to live out a happy life in Seville. I love the city's vitality and the contrast between the mad pageantry in the streets and the civilized pace of the daily round. No one here has to be reminded to stop and smell the roses. Every spring, when Seville's orange blossoms fill the air with the sweet scent known as *azahar*, everyone goes around sniffing and smiling for weeks.

As of this writing, it's been nearly eleven years since Rich and I first visited Seville and six and a half years since we chose to live here. By now I've mastered enough Spanish to hold my own in just about any situation, including nights out on the town, philosophical debates, business meetings, telephone complaints, and price negotiations with *butaneros*. On a good day, I can even toss out the *subjuntivo* in causal conversation. I still miss a lot of double entendres and *palabras verdes* ("green words," meaning curses and obscenities), but perhaps that's just as well. As Rich points out, if we can't understand what motorists are yelling from a passing car, we can remain in blissful ignorance, assuming that it has nothing to do with us or that they're wishing us a long and joyful life out of a general sense of bonhomie.

We've renewed the lease on our apartment for another five years and obtained our permanent Spanish residency cards. We still make our twice-yearly visits to San Anselmo, which is now comfortingly familiar and just zany enough to keep me entertained. Seville, on the other hand, is where I live out loud: I sing in the streets, throw flower petals at the Blessed Virgin, dance in the fountain, pretend to believe ham lowers my cholesterol, stay up until dawn, and always stop to smell the *azahar*. Seville is life in full, wide-screen, Technicolor glory, with a soundtrack provided by flamenco singers, accordion-playing gypsies, Handel's *Messiah* in the cathedral, and brass bands in the streets.

I was forty-nine years old when I first set foot in Seville, and I just celebrated my sixtieth birthday here. Living abroad has built a lot of vivid memories and, with luck, is keeping my brain sharp enough to recall at least most of them. Dividing my time between what's-happening-now California and one of Europe's ancient cities keeps me on my mental toes. I am constantly surprised, confused, fooled, intrigued, and charmed by the world around me. I'm not sleepwalking through the years on my way to God's waiting room.

American friends and relatives are always asking me how long I'm planning to stay here; of course, what they really want to know is when I will come to my senses and return home. I explain that I *am* home. Seville is where my heart is. But if I've learned anything over the years and many moves, it's never to say never. Some personal, family, or world crisis might compel me to return to the US, or some new adventure might entice me to live somewhere else. The great thing about life is its sublime unpredictability.

So I suppose the truest answer is, I don't know how long I'll be here.

But then, does anyone?

Reading Group Guide

DANCING *in the* FOUNTAIN

How to Enjoy Living Abroad

Karen McCann

READING GROUP GUIDE

Questions and Topics for Discussion

1. Karen says she and her husband moved to Seville because they didn't want to "just soldier on for a while and then sit around waiting to crumble." Is that a good enough reason? Do you think that's the real reason? What would it take to motivate you to make such a major move?

2. If you could spend a year anywhere in the world, where would you go?

3. If you were moving to a foreign country, what possessions would you take with you? What would be hardest to leave behind?

4. What are some of the benefits and drawbacks to the time of life the McCanns chose for embarking on such a major change?

5. Were you surprised by Karen's friends' reactions to the announcement they were moving to Seville? How do you think you'd react to a similar announcement by a close friend?

6. How do the McCanns' experiences in Cleveland and California sharpen their appreciation of Seville? Do you think having homes in two countries would make living abroad easier or more difficult?

7. What are some of the qualities of Spanish life that contrast most sharply with your own culture? Which aspects of the Sevillano lifestyle did Karen and Rich actively incorporate into their own lives? Which aspects would you have been drawn to?

8. What frustrations did the McCanns encounter while learning Spanish? Have you ever struggled to communicate in another language?

9. If you were living in Spain, would you go to a bullfight? Why or why not?

10. Karen talks about the importance of "mentally unpacking your bags." Why is this so essential when moving anywhere, and especially abroad?

11. Have you ever had difficult houseguests or visitors who overstayed their welcome? What are some strategies for coping with awkward guests?

12. In *Eat, Pray, Love*, Elizabeth Gilbert's friend declares that every city – and every person – can be described by a single word. Rome's is "sex," the Vatican's is "power." Gilbert declares New York's to be "achieve" but later chooses "*antevasin*," Sanskrit for "one who lives at the border." What word would you use for Seville?

For more on Karen McCann and Dancing in the Fountain visit
EnjoyLivingAbroad.com
facebook.com/EnjoyLivingAbroad
twitter.com/EnjoyLvngAbroad

CPSIA information can be obtained at www.ICGtesting.com
Printed in the USA
BVOW01s0200181214

379945BV00001B/84/P